RESONANT CORPORATIONS

# RESONANT CORPORATIONS

Marc van der Erve

**McGraw-Hill**
New York   San Francisco   Washington, D.C.   Auckland   Bogotá
Caracas   Lisbon   London   Madrid   Mexico City   Milan
Montreal   New Delhi   San Juan   Singapore
Sydney   Tokyo   Toronto

## McGraw-Hill

*A Division of The McGraw-Hill Companies*

1 2 3 4 5 6 7 8 9 0   DOC/DOC   9 0 2 1 0 9 8 7

ISBN 0-07-067037-4

McGraw-Hill books are available at special quantity discounts to use as premiums and sales promotions, or for use in corporate training programs. For more information, please write to the Director of Special Sales, McGraw-Hill, 11 West 19th Street, New York, NY 10011. Or contact your local bookstore.

# *A*CKNOWLEDGEMENTS

SOCIETY IS A LABORATORY of observers and the observed. I would like to acknowledge those people who have contributed knowingly and unknowingly to a decade of research into the behavior of people, organizations and how they create and manage business.

One group of people, in particular, deserves to be mentioned: the growth conditions survey participants. Executives in 109 companies were willing to share their personal views on the conditions in their organizations. They also contributed to an insight into the ideas about corrective measures which still influence the actions of most if not all executives. I thank these executives for their contribution to this survey.

I would also like to acknowledge Sabin Azua Mendia, Remko Renes, Gerard Scholte, Martijn van der Erve and, in particular, my wife Karen.

ABOUT THE AUTHOR—Marc van der Erve, founder of Evolution Management Corporation, is an established researcher, consultant and trainer. He is the author of several leading books on the theme of corporate dynamics, including *Evolution Management* and *The Power of Tomorrow's Management*. With Jonathan Ellis he wrote a novel, *The Darwin Circle*. He is the developer of an integrated approach for business renewal, social engineering and benchmarking, all of which are supported by advanced Windows 95-based software. He has used this "computer-based training" approach in many consulting assignments.

Marc van der Erve received a cum laude degree in applied physics. After having followed a post-graduate management program at Insead in France, he earned a doctorate in organizational sociology at Tilburg University in The Netherlands. He is member of the Society for the Advancement of Socio-Economics (SASE) in the United States.

Marc van der Erve has been an advisor to a variety of distinguished organizations and agencies such as PTT Telecom, the European Free Trade Association (EFTA), Winterthur Insurance, Roche Pharma (Switzerland), Secura Insurance, The Baloise and KPMG Management Consultants. His E-mail address is: marc.vandererve@skynet.be

# CONTENTS

# RESONANT CORPORATIONS

*To Karen*

*All growth is a leap in the dark, a spontaneous unpremeditated*
*act without benefit of experience.*
            Henry Miller

# PROLOGUE

THIS BOOK is intended for an "endangered species:" Entrepreneurs and managers—plus the professionals in their organizations—who, unless they take action now, will discover that they have run out of time.

The emphasis in most companies is probably already shifting away from cost-cutting and the improvement of business processes toward the search for new growth. And in this search for new growth, many managers try to emulate the conditions prevalent in other high growth situations. Too late they discover this doesn't work. In fact, an international growth conditions survey—the results of which have been incorporated in this book—indicates that this is actually counterproductive. What's more, the crisp rules for market leadership which have been reiterated in so many best-selling books prove equally ineffective in this new situation. For while every individual in an organization may approve of these rules, the organization as a whole is often incapable of following them through.

A new approach is needed which mobilizes the hidden knowledge and energy found both inside and outside organizations. An approach which focuses the search on characteristics (of people, situations, customers, products, competencies, partners and attitudes) that reinforce one another. Characteristics that resonate.

This book explores how growth can be achieved through resonance and analyzes the most appropriate conditions. The starting-points are so fundamental, that some philosophical consequences have also invited examination. These are often centered on the constant dynamics of business organizations and go beyond cultural differences; they are therefore likely to attract more views on the development of growth. Thus, the study of the inception and decay of business may very well develop into a new discipline which could be referred to as "natural economics." That does not mean that the search for new growth in business is turning into a science. Business organizations will always need "naturals" who have developed the gift of sensing and realizing business opportunities; I hope this book may help others to develop such "natural" senses too. Its brief chapters present what has been learned from studies in business management and in the behavioral sciences about how people can best build and maintain a business organization. They include the wisdom of people in many companies. The idea has been to explain the conditions and measures that allow people to produce valuable results.

Although you will probably experience your read as a journey through new territory, I trust you will gain practical knowledge from this book and share it with others in your organization. May it help you to achieve growth in business and life.

*Always Be Prepared
To Put Everything In
Perspective*

*Failure, Success,
Assumptions, Expressions,
Written And
Unwritten Rules*

\*

*Civilization is a movement and not a condition,*
*a voyage and not a harbour.*
              A. J. Toynbee

# DIVINE RULES

A GOOD RELATIONSHIP depends on people being on the same wavelength. It doesn't mean that you have to agree with someone on each and every detail but, rather, that your views, your thoughts, somehow reinforce those of the other person. When thoughts reinforce one another, they resonate. And, when they do, so do behaviors. This is exactly what makes and breaks good teams. Resonating thoughts and behaviors, both good and bad, are the underpinnings of families, organizations, business, movements and even societies.

Under certain circumstances, however, resonance can have a devastating effect. In 1940, four months after it was completed, the suspension bridge which spanned the Narrows south-east of New York began to sway dangerously in sweeping gales. In the mid-section, the vibrations somehow accumulated (resonance) until the bridge literally moved like a snake between the intermediate supports and anchors at either end. Ultimately, when the undulations became uncontrollable, the bridge collapsed.

In (business) society, dramatic undulations may also occur. They are often caused by "mental anchors."

During a heated discussion about the inner drive of people in business, I was reminded of one of the main mental anchors in business society. My discussion partner pointed at a circle that he had just drawn and said: "This is God… or the equivalent of God for those who don't believe." Then he drew a bigger circle around it. "Those are our basic virtues, like love, hope, trust and so on." He drew yet another concentric circle around the previous two. He looked up mysteriously and said: "Those are our values. They depend on our basic virtues and bring to the surface certain rules, strategies and decisions."

However much sense these observations made, they evoked feelings in me much like those that must have overwhelmed Galileo Galilei in his confrontation with the Church in 1633. In my mind's eye, I saw the concentric circles swell into planets and stars, all of which seemed to revolve around the earth. I was looking at a representation of a divine universe, a medieval framework of reference. But it does not only put the deity in the middle; man, as a predestined deity in his dreams, is right at the center as well. It dawned on me that this simple drawing still represents the core of today's thinking on how we should tackle (business) challenges. It might explain our relentless search for eternal corporate life and those grandiose visions which express our longing for an unimaginable increase in sophistication, complexity, growth and power. Can this be why we tend to explain evolution as "development for the better," whatever that better may mean?

Although we have benefited immensely from this mental anchor, it tends to bring about a rather egocentric view which narrows our choice and prevents our gaze from moving to new places. To new universes of understanding. As we see in so many places in our world, when forces eventually accumulate, mental anchors cause uncontrollable undulations and, in the end, collapse.

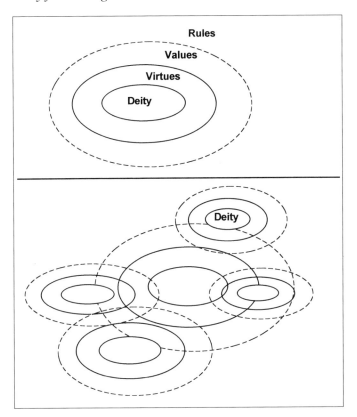

*A broader perspective in business and society requires us to move away
from a concentric world to a complex, interacting world of worlds.
A key question is: "How does resonance hold everything together?"*

Mental anchors also play an important role in business society.
But just like the bridge, resonance—the reinforcement of behaviors—eventually forces organizations to detach themselves from
them. And so although mental anchors may seem to be the pillars
of success, resonance is its true dynamic resource. A decade of
research points quite clearly to this unfamiliar perspective. The

intention of this book is to review the learning points that broaden the spectrum from which we develop and choose business rules.

### *Beyond the Traditional Starting-Point*

This task is essentially different from other attempts to describe the conditions for corporate growth. Traditionally, the work of numerous management experts and publicly acclaimed gurus starts from the very thing at which the corporate world is aiming: success. It becomes the number one mental anchor. Typically, management experts roamed the world of corporate heavyweights interviewing top management to lay bare the divine rules that made these companies successful. The brilliance of the resulting classification work and the effect it had on the corporate world should not be underestimated. But, however necessary, useful and perceptive such case-studies may have been, they have left gaps in the validity and credibility of the rules that were recommended. Some examples of corporate success "failed" miserably when they exhausted their growth potential. And so the studies continue. Different examples of success reveal new sets of rules. Yet the starting-point remains the same. Where there is smoke, there is fire. Where there is success, there are rules.

Again we are walking in the footsteps of Galileo—for to question this belief is to question established thinking. Yet question it we must. First, the starting-point of success is debatable. After all, what is success? How do we quantify it? What do we use as a benchmark? Second, the underlying assumptions are still predominantly divine. The remains of a religious past cause us to place management and organizations within a subconscious framework which probably overvalues the divine role of the human race. Third, because there are so many ways to achieve success, the supply of divine rules has swollen far beyond the digestive capacity of managers. The incredible number of rules and the even more impressive number of examples makes it virtually impossible for anyone to select the rules which best fit the company or situation. It is simply not realistic to assume that managers have the time and energy to internalize a mega-summary of success examples.

*Fatal Attraction*
In 1996, Microsoft seemed to keep both feet on the ground when enjoying the succes of its new PC operating system and product lines. It rapidly aligned itself to the sudden emergence of Internet as a phenomenon which might determine the information technology business of tomorrow. As we know all too well, the mental anchor of success has an almost fatal attraction which either generates the energy to achieve it or drives someone over the top into counter-productive behavior. Companies like Apple, IBM and Digital have tasted success until they were drowned by it. They pursued increasing performance goals and growth at the cost of their capacity to react effectively to inevitable trends in the industry. This behavior is not unfamiliar to most companies. Apparently, we do not sufficiently realize that, even in stable times after the war, about one-half of the Fortune Five-Hundred either disappeared altogether or dropped out of the front ranks within a period of 25 years.

So what is success in a rapidly changing world? And which conditions does today's manager think will sustain it when business evolves? These two questions are fundamental issues and must be addressed very seriously. This is essential, for the research findings in this book indicate that the perceptions of most managers on these matters differ from those of today's outstanding entrepreneurs. The average manager—unlike the successful entrepreneur—has narrowed his view of success to reflect only one particular phase of the corporate life cycle.

Therefore, rather than using success as the origin of business rules, this book focuses on "movement"—that is, from "where an organization is now" to "where it will be in the future." The idea is to derive rules from an unfolding process rather than from a disputable end-state. To describe such a process requires an understanding of the basic forces which cause "movement" and access to the reservoir of insights created by a whole host of scientific disciplines. The main challenge is to bring these insights together into a social logic which more accurately describes the evolution of business organizations.

You are now embarking on a journey right into the heart of a black hole—a journey which is almost certain to generate a sense of disintegration as the established paradigm, our framework of reference in life, is torn apart until only floating concepts are left. Yet, as Stephen Hawking predicts, a black hole ends in a "wormhole" which functions as a passage to another universe. This new universe may seem very much like our own. But it differs in that it is based on a new understanding of the origin of growth in business. It contains a dynamic framework of reference, a "logic of movement," which may help us to reinterpret our role in the evolution of business organizations.

*Are your people on the same wavelength?*

*Do you sense that their behaviors reinforce ane another?*

*Which mental anchors are you consciously or subconsciously using?*

*Can you distinguish the mental anchors that are blocking new insights?*

*Whose mental anchors mainly block new insights, yours or your people's?*

*To what degree does "success," as you know it, block new insights and initiatives?*

*Should you lay down rules or try to establish directions first?*

*What is your considered opinion of the organizational purpose?*

*And what is your purpose within this purpose?*

*Do Not Be Blinded By Revolution*

*Focus On Changes Inside and Outside Your Organization Which Might Reinforce One Another*

*

*The day is not far off when the economic problem will take the back seat where it belongs, and the arena of the heart and the head will be occupied or reoccupied, by our real problems: the problems of life and of human relations, of creation and behaviour.*
John Maynard Keynes

## MAD INTERACTION

NEAR THE END of his presentation on key threats in the electronics market, C. K. Prahalad, renowned for his research on core competencies, summed up the sources of performance for Philips' management. Four stages running from the 1960's right into the next millennium all had one remarkable "source" in common. It was the last item listed in each stage. And it was quite simply luck. Although at first glance it seemed to be an insignificant item, radiating very little scientific or business credibility, luck was, in fact, the most valuable piece of information on that slide.

What makes luck so pertinent? It has to do with the unpredictability of present business life. Today's business world is complex. Economies are becoming more and more intertwined—a process which foments unbridled interaction. A growing number of interactions, fueled by technological developments which dramatically increase our capacity to communicate and trade, make the exact outcome of our initiatives increasingly unpredictable. Such unpredictability—Prahalad's luck—insults our sense of control. We can no longer sit back and trust some proven method or past success to guide us into the future. The "chance-driven" process of evolution which apparently rules our business world produces new opportunities. But it does so at the cost of certainty. It forces industries, corporations, organizations and also individuals to maintain a state of alertness which is essential if they are to react appropriately to unprecedented developments in a continuously changing landscape of events.

---

*Interaction Defuses Generalizations*

The developments in various industries seem to contradict one another and defuse some of the generalizations about the trends in business society. In reaction to regulatory and technological change, for example, AT&T abandoned vertical integration and decided to break up the company into three separate units. For just the same reasons, Walt Disney and Capital Cities/ABC, a few months before, decided to merge. Also, Ford acquired the ownership of Herz car rentals while it made sense for General Motors to spin off EDS at the time. As the *Financial Times* observes, broad generalizations about integration versus specialization or conglomeration versus focus seem worthless. Interaction means the rules are different for everyone. Everything depends on the pressures affecting individual industries and, within them, the different circumstances of the companies themselves. Mad interaction, therefore, forces us to search at other levels for a logic that may explain the appearance and disappearance of spontaneous order in business society.

---

Since the nineteenth century, the strength of the French railways has declined—an inevitable consequence of the growth of car travel, the rise of individualism and the evolution of society. The train strikes which paralyzed the country in 1995 could not prevent drastic reforms to the industry. It shows that, as business develops and spontaneous order emerges, there is only room for those organizations and rules that fit in with the evolving landscape. Those that fail to fit in are altered—often unwillingly—or simply disappear. Any attempt to halt evolution through an act of desperation turns out to be futile. The ruthless process of selection which Darwin identified gropes around in a bubbling soup of events in which order of any kind appears and vanishes spontaneously. Sophistication of traits does not win favor. Selection and survival depends only on whether the traits fit in with the dynamic landscape of interactions. This explains why the bold rather than the beautiful sometimes survive. Or, in the eyes of Apple computer fans, why Apple computers lost out to those that were Intel-based.

The evolution of society and business can unfold with lightning speed when sequences of tiny but nonetheless rapid changes take place at the same time and cause a new order to appear. When these seemingly unrelated changes interact and reinforce one another (when they resonate), a revolution of some kind is felt. Take the Internet: it may very well be remembered as the revolution of the late 'nineties—a spontaneous order which seemed to have emerged overnight. But this will betray its true origins. For people may well forget that its roots go back to the early 'seventies when the U.S. Department of Defense set up a network, ARPAnet, to connect various military and research sites. When industry, eager to attract business, gradually joined this network, the Internet grew. The creation of the hypertext-based WorldWideWeb by scientists at the European Laboratory for Particle Physics in Geneva, followed by the introduction of Internet browser software, eventually helped to light the fuse of Internet's explosive growth.

In today's business world, planning still attempts to impose predictability on something which is essentially unpredictable in outcome. And in this environment, adaptation becomes a hoax. The word "adaptation" means "to make fit for a specific situation." It belongs to the teleological vocabulary which presumes that the order and efficiency of the natural world are not accidental. It reflects views of divine leadership and destiny which have molded our perception of control. Of course, once organizations have changed, they seem to have "adapted." Unbridled interaction, however, causes constant, unexpected movement rather than adaptation because the situation to which they were adapting at the start of the process will have changed by the end of it. The 1995 Nobel Prize-winner in Economics, Robert Lucas, reinvented dynamic economic theory based on this phenomenon. Since the expectations of people and their behavior change in time, he reasoned, government policies may not yield the anticipated results. Government policies are, of necessity, based on the past behavior of people; the response when they are finally implemented is likely to be different from what is expected. Economic models, as a result, now incorporate assessments of how people's expectations may change—in other words, projections of future economic landscapes. They forecast how economic signals might develop through time in a complex, unpredictable environment.

### Beyond the Signals Toward Creation

In our attempts to control the future, we have been drawn into the interpretation of signals. Using models of the feedback type, we compare the outcomes of our actions with our goals, and thus we lash ourselves with signals from the past to re-conceptualize our world. Our behavior resembles reading the Koran which literally stands for "recitation." Our preoccupation with the explanation of signals narrows our framework of reference to fundamentalist concepts which have mainly been inspired by previous success and failure. As a result, the understanding of "learning" has decomposed into the elements of differentiation and transmission. The latter, in particular, has been overemphasized. Learning also refers to movement on an unexpected path of change and, as brain research indicates, this is a physiological characteristic of learning. In other words, learning is the experience and interpretation of the unknown. In cultural evolution, transmission refers to the communication of signals in broad feedback loops; differentiation, however, which deals with "becoming different, distinct or more specialized," hints at "creation." Unbridled interaction and the resulting growth in the number of spontaneous types of order that arise in (business) society make differentiation a central issue. The familiar interpretation of learning, therefore, needs to be augmented through a stronger emphasis on differentiation and creation.

*The Domain of Mad Interaction*
- *Selection*—A ruthless process in which survival depends on developments which fit the evolving environment.
- *Revolution*—A term invented to explain "sudden events" which occur when gradual developments reinforce one another.
- *Adaptation*—A hoax when planning predictably to adjust what is unpredictable in outcome. Adaptation can only be "movement".
- *Learning*—The experience and interpretation of the unknown. It decays into differentiation and transmission.
- *Natural Economics*—The study of creation and decay through the forces and directions of "movement" in business society.

The sheer number of interacting events in the business environment, the sense of constant movement rather than adaptation and the need to differentiate in the crowded business scene all dramatically affect the way we plan for future business. Industries, corporations, situations and rules arise unexpectedly and we are forced to develop scenarios of spontaneous order in business which at first glance appear unbelievable. In the 'seventies, for example, Royal Dutch/Shell gained a competitive advantage when its master planner, Pierre Wack, followed such an approach to arrive at a surprising 20-fold price increase per barrel of oil.

The study of the process of inception and decay of spontaneous order in business is only in its infancy. It deals with the scarcity of opportunities in the dynamic business landscape and so feeds on economics. But, as we shall discuss further on in this book, the dynamic forces of creation come from beyond traditional economic signals and have been identified both in social and natural sciences. Therefore, if this study deserves its own label, I suggest referring to it as "natural economics." Natural economics explains how people eventually come to cling together and evolve as a whole, as a social order. It aims to describe the process of creation and decay by exploring the forces and directions of movement in business society. It is relevant in our business world where mad interaction is likely to cause the next millennium to be characterized by constant movement.

After our first leap into the dark in which we have raised questions about matters of common sense, we are ready to continue our exploration. In his study on the origin of biological species, Darwin based his findings on traces of organisms in sedimentary rock. Similarly, we will search for "traces of growth" in business.

*What is evolution? If it is progress,
then what is progress?*

*If evolution is concerned with the interaction of events,
then what can you do about it?*

*Which matters tell you something about
the process of evolution?*

*Should you be driven by signals of the past
or by tomorrow's situations?*

*How should you interpret "survival"
when your organization takes on
a different form with a different purpose?*

*In your organization, how can you build up
confidence to face the unknown?*

*What should you do about the injustice of
natural selection in which change is driven
more by chance than excellence?*

*What should the role of a leader be in
organizations that do not adapt
but merely change?*

*There Is Only So Much Growth
You Can Squeeze Out Of
Organizations In Their Lifetime*

*New Sources of Growth Require
New Organizations With
Growth Potential Of Their Own*

*People Are The Seeds Of
Future Growth*

\*

*What is the most rigorous law of our being? Growth. No smallest atom of our moral, mental, or physical structure can stand still a year. It grows—it must grow; nothing can prevent it.*
Mark Twain

## WOBBLES OF GROWTH

Hᴏᴡ ᴍᴀɴʏ ᴛɪᴍᴇꜱ have you said that quality not quantity is important? And how many times would you have to admit to yourself that your final judgment was nevertheless based on quantity? Quantity does not necessarily say anything about quality, yet it can still be meaningful as a measure of growth.

Once, in a management seminar about growth, I used a provocative example first identified by Cesare Marchetti and later evaluated in a captivating way by Theodore Modis, a growth dynamics researcher. The example refers to the growth in the number of compositions which Wolfgang Amadeus Mozart (1756–91) and Johannes Brahms (1833–97) published during their lifetime. Mozart, who wrote for a living, produced close to 600 catalogued compositions. He wrote his first piece when he was six and died at the age of 35 at which time his creative potential (in terms of number of compositions) came to an end after less than 30 years. Brahms, who wrote for pleasure, published "only" 126 catalogued musical compositions and died at the age of 64. As in all cases of "natural growth," the number of compositions plotted by year follow a bell-shaped curve or a tilted S-curve when plotting the cumulative numbers. These typical contours show growth starting slowly, then increasing rapidly, before subsiding at the end. Both composers died, Modis claims, when approaching the theoretical end of their growth curve.

Before I could finish my story, the audience, much to my surprise, reacted in disbelief. "This is quite impossible," one listener expostulated. "Why should someone die when they reach the end of their growth curve?" It took me a moment to realize why they objected to a phenomenon which can be observed in most forms of growth—whether growth in revenue, in quality improvements, in the use of nuclear energy, in the spread of diseases or in creativity. Apparently, some of the students in the room were at turning points in their careers. The MBA program, of which my seminar was part, marked the beginning of a subsequent phase in their lives. It occurred to me that, in their eyes, this example destroyed their futures. Their concerns, however, ebbed when we examined Mozart's case.

Mozart concentrated on one type of output. "Normal" people

---

*Magic Behind Survival and Growth?*

What is the magic behind survival and growth? Is it grand vision? Bill Hewlett, one of the two founders of Hewlett-Packard, devastated management experts when he said: "We were succesful because we had *no* plans." Is it, then, the open and informal Hewlett-Packard way? Well, if that is the case, how can we explain why the Roman Catholic Church and the Swedish company Stora have endured for centuries? Also, an obsession with growth tends to limit rather than help companies. When blindly pursuing growth, Digital Equipment Corporation, although in some respects similar to Hewlett-Packard, became insensitive to its surroundings and lost out to its archrival. Apparently, organizationss survive and generate growth for reasons at which, for the moment, we can only guess.

tend to have more than just one type of output, although none, generally, as impressive as Mozart's. This is also true in business society. Some companies and organizations achieve one magnificent bubble of growth—and then vanish. Others are capable of regenerating themselves time and again. Hewlett-Packard is an extraordinary example of the latter. It found its first niche in the production of electronic measuring equipment and then progressed into a growing number of different product lines.

From a natural growth perspective, Mozart and Brahms differ in the total number of catalogued compositions they produced and the stretch of time each needed to write them. Mozart's growth curve, compared with Brahms', rose steeply and reached a very much higher level. Given the differences in constitution and situation, it would have been impossible to turn Brahms into "a Mozart." Growth potential—that is the rate and ceiling of growth—is a characteristic of someone's constitution in a specific environment. Also, in business, it is unlikely that we can significantly alter the life cycle and growth expectations of organizations. Organizations fulfill their typical growth potential but are, at the same time, limited by it. Once growth occurs, on-going survival depends on the creation of new "life forms" or spontaneous order.

### Birthplace of Growth

In 1996, the Dutch-based aircraft manufacturer Fokker filed for bankruptcy. For several years at the start of the 'eighties it had been marked by stagnating growth and so, inspired by a dominant "corporate messiah," it worked on the development of a new main source of revenue: its F-100 aircraft. In the same pre-1987 period, however, the fate of Fokker was already seen to be linked to that of the US dollar. When the dollar continued its decline, Fokker's bankruptcy became unavoidable. Neither its considerable growth nor the cash injections from its new owner and benefactor DASA,

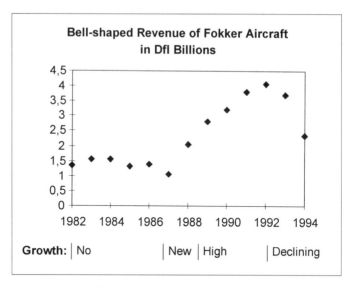

*A wobble of growth represents a yardstick of corporate inception and decay. It unfolds in four distinct phases:* no growth, new growth, high growth *and* declining growth.

the German Aerospace concern of Daimler-Benz, could prevent its demise. Actually, the underpinnings of corporate life and demise had been already created during the period of stagnating growth. In hindsight, the dollar value represented the evolving fitness landscape. Ultimately, growth potential is locked into the early complexity of organizational design and how it fits the evolving environment.

The ragged growth of revenue is often perceived as a scent of decay. A company, of course, will disintegrate when it fails to identify viable sources of growth. The conditions for survival may simply not be in place. A slackening growth, however, may also signal the potential for new growth. An organization in this stage might well be waiting for someone or certain conditions to recondition it and light its fuse. Companies such as Israel's biggest and most profitable holding group, Koor Industries, use this principle. They buy industry equity and bring in management and technology to identify and develop new sources of growth. Then, when growth emerges, they float the companies on the local market. This approach hints at a logic for procreation in business society.

### Yardstick of Inception and Decay

Once revenue grows and can be sustained, a period of high growth follows. Driven by the need to materialize their revenue growth potential as efficiently as possible, organizations become integration-oriented. Operational links with suppliers, business partners and customers are forged so that the flow of information and goods along the supply line runs more smoothly. Organizations also begin an internal integration of processes and systems. When the focus on operational links prevails, the sensitivity of organizations to fundamental changes in the market is traded in for the development of a corporate "mechanism" dedicated to the realization of growth.

Integration is essential in stages of high growth; when growth declines or halts, however, it becomes counterproductive. A continued drive toward integration narrows the focus and inhibits the inner forces and freedom needed for the development of new sources of growth. Eventually, when growth declines further and companies fail to meet expectations, organizations inevitably fragment as functions such as sales, manufacturing and product development start to shift the blame onto each other.

The growth conditions survey, which has been conducted in support of the avenues explored here, confirms the pendulum shift in emphasis between integration and fragmentation. The opinions reveal the most fitting or natural organizational states by phase of growth. Integration is best in situations of high growth and, to

[ 25 ]

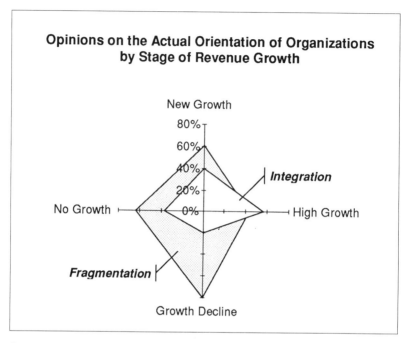

**Opinions on the Actual Orientation of Organizations by Stage of Revenue Growth**

*In each stage of growth, the opinions of the actual orientation of organizations show the state which has survived the evolutionary process of selection. Integration is only functional in a stage of high growth, while fragmentation, more than integration, benefits progress in all other stages. When asked for their preference, managers mistakenly chose for integration as the only model of reference in all stages of growth.*

a lesser extent, when new growth emerges. Fragmentation, however, dominates in three of the four stages of growth. When growth declines, and especially when there is no growth at all, organizational fragmentation—not integration—is imperative. Of course, in the search for new sources of output, the growing number of organizational fragments increases the probability of their inception.

When asked what they would prefer in each state of growth, managers submitted answers which revealed that they had been misled by the popular trend to integrate. The evidence overwhelmingly shows that managers would prefer to strive for integration rather than fragmentation in all stages of growth. High growth is the model of reference, probably because it is associated with harvest-time. Declining growth, no growth and, to a certain extent, new growth are seen as failure. Apparently, managers, unlike entrepreneurs, are confined to a predictable world where strategy is a matter of biased extrapolation and not renewal. Their notion of success, therefore, must stem from the stage of high growth and its typical state of integration. This unfortunate misconception about the roots of progress—this rather primitive view of success—indicates that the logic of evolution and, in particular, the process of inception and renewal are not yet sufficiently appreciated.

*Uncovering Perceptions and Misconceptions*
The growth conditions survey was conducted to identify the organizational states and directions which have evolved naturally and to explore the perceptions or misconceptions of management. The survey covers 131 generally high-level managers in 109 corporations across seven countries in Europe. The contributing corporations include profit and non-profit organizations in a wide variety of industries. Tests indicated that the opinions of managers in the various countries do not differ significantly. The outcome of this survey will be referred to throughout this book. It underlines the philosophy of natural economics that is discussed here and sheds light on the phenomenon of movement in society.

Through its distinct and recurrent phases of development, growth enables us to transform the arrow of time into a yardstick of corporate inception and decay. Although it is useful as a measuring-stick which helps us to trace the forces of organizational life, natural growth remains just a "signal" of evolution. It does not sufficiently expose the true background of movement nor the conditions for survival.

*What key phenomena in your company
seem to be subject to growth?*

*Where does your organization seem to pursue
growth blindly?*

*To what extent are the institutions in your organization
driven by expectations of eternal life?*

*Should your people challenge the very things
that make your organization successful?*

*Should lack of growth be forgiven when the experience
is used to develop growth alternatives?*

*How should your organization anticipate decay
and the need for inception when it is experiencing
healthy growth?*

*What do you need to do to make your organization
understand that another wobble of growth may
force it to be dramatically different?*

*People, Organizations
And Cultures Are Driven By
The Need For Autonomy
And Interdependence*

*Which Need Is Dominant
And Who Is In Sync?*

\*

*Any consideration of the life and larger social existence of the*
*modern corporate man begins and also largely ends with the effect*
*of one all-embracing force. That is organization.*
John Kenneth Galbraith

# DAWNING OF MOVEMENT

IN THE SECOND HALF of the 'eighties, in *The Power of Tomorrow's Management* (1989), I examined how the effectiveness of attitudes changes in sync with the development of growth in organizations along its typical wobble-like or tilted S-curve outlines. Attitudes change in certain directions in one particular stage of growth and in opposite directions in another. Based on these shifts, the corporate structure and rules can be adjusted to create favorable conditions for progress or survival. Because my work relates the changing complexity of an organization to the phenomenon of growth, it was included in the book *Predictions* by Theodore Modis. I coined the term "culture engineering" to label the necessary adjustment of organizational rules by management which eventually affects the corporate values. This is probably why my book earned a comment from the noted Amitai Etzioni, founder of *The Communitarian Network* and various other social movements. At the time, however, my assessment was limited to the "mechanics" of change and did not sufficiently touch upon the basic question: "Why?"

In the years that followed, I worked on refinements which enable one to anticipate future organizational states based on qualitative assessments. Eventually, my understanding of the evolution of organizations was ready to benefit from a phenomenon which lies at the core of "movement" in society: self-organizing behavior. It is a fundamental characteristic of physical, biological and social orders to generate the internal drive which changes their own complexity or structure. It must have been a case of mad inter-action that, at the time, I met Gilbert Probst who, in my view, deserves to be qualified as historian of the phenomenon of self-organization. My encounter with Probst in 1992 coincided with the death of Friedrich von Hayek, the renowned economist and one of the first to identify the self-organizing behavior of social orders. With Etzioni, who once asked the question: "How can an organization change itself better to fulfill its values?," von Hayek and, also, Probst appear on a long list of scholars who brought the notion of self-organizing behavior to the surface.

### Evidence of Internally Driven Change

In the human brain and a collection of brains, such as an organiza-tion, signals from outside do not necessarily result in a noticeable response. And this is fortunate. Imagine what would happen to a football player in a stadium full of supporters if he were to react to each and every signal. A football player follows his own mind, so to speak, which reacts to events only when it considers them relevant. The brain and an organization both depend on an internal drift which determines their activities. This drift ensures that priorities are continually traced and set—a process which causes gradual changes to the structure. In organizations, a trace of this drift is visible in the structural changes that mark their evolution.

When growth develops, the sensitivity of an organization to its environment varies in time. For example, when an organization is in search for demand, it generates changes to its structure which open it up to potential customers and their evolving needs. Once a kernel of marketable products has been identified, an organization then seals itself off to dedicate its activities to the establishment of processes which will ensure the most efficient delivery of these products. This "closure" is compensated by opening up operations to link internal processes with those of suppliers and

*Traces of Internally Driven Change*

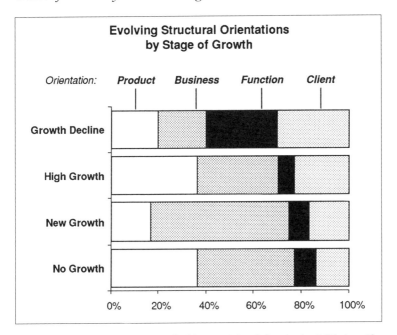

*In the opinion survey, evidence of self-organizing behavior is visible in self-induced structural change in successive stages of revenue growth. When experiencing new growth, organizations are mainly structured around the business, e.g. in the form of business units. When high growth emerges, organizations seem to assume a product orientation to realize rapid revenue growth across various business units. When growth declines, function-based structures are pursued to correct the problem operationally. When the decline in growth persists, however, companies tend to focus their organizations on client segments hoping to identify their hidden needs.*

customers and, in this way, to improve the overall efficiency. The continuing drive to realize its growth potential causes an organization to vary its closure by changing its structure from time to time.

The growth conditions survey confirmed the anticipated structural changes. In pursuit of momentum and efficiency, organizations move from business-based to product-based structures when growth accelerates. When growth stagnates, they pursue functional structures to regain control of growth and to squeeze more juice from the corporate lemon. When growth cannot be restored and continues to decline, organizations change the structure yet again to suit the market landscape, hoping to uncover evolving customer needs and new pockets of growth.

Internally driven change is limited by the capacity of organizations to change. Once they have exhausted their natural growth potential, organizations are no longer able to adjust to the environment without compromising their core identity. At that point, they are forced to break away from their trusted image.

Now that we have evidence of self-organizing behavior how can we explain it?

### *Toward a Framework of Movement*

Self-organizing behavior emerges only when certain conditions are satisfied. As the Japanese politician Ichiro Ozawa observes: "[It] begins with the autonomy of the individual." Autonomy is one of the main conditions of self-organizing behavior. It turns up everywhere. In countries, the success of regions is related to autonomous control of finance and technology. In industry, the creation of more autonomous units tends to increase efficiency and a company's capacity to react to changing circumstances. Thanks to autonomous units, change, which is then less restrained by inertia, can spread more quickly throughout an organization, attracting innovative points of view along the way. Autonomy, in this way, triggers the need to orchestrate organizational units so that their actions reinforce one another. It is a characteristic which determines the relationship between the organization as a whole and its elements. Not surprisingly, it leads to "complexity."

Complexity, a darling topic at some of today's conferences on management, is another key condition of self-organizing behavior. In biological systems, complexity is essential for self-organization. In his study of evolution, the French priest, paleontologist, and philosopher Teilhard de Chardin (1881–1955) related the growing complexity of the brain to the emergence of consciousness. Organizations also need to become more complex before self-organizing behavior develops. But what is complexity?

---

*Autonomy and Interdependencies*

By increasing the autonomy of suppliers within its manufacturing operations, Volkswagen has become remarkably efficient while maintaining its capacity to adjust to changing circumstances. In its Brazilian factories, production is done by suppliers. The workers of suppliers actually pre-assemble modular components inside the plants. Similarly, Compaq, the personal computer maker, increased its flexibility, efficiency and the quality of its products by devolving autonomy to so-called "manufacturing cells." Cell manufacturing has given the company tremendous flexibility in adjusting to short-term fluctuations in demand. Even the success of Europe's most prosperous regions, such as Baden-Württemberg, Catalonia, Lombardy and Rhônes Alpes, has been attributed to their autonomy in controlling finance and technology. As a study by Lorange and Probst confirms, the lack of autonomy is one of the main reasons why most joint ventures fail. By devolution, change is delegated to organizational elements each of which can react faster then the whole. Autonomy invites balance by measures which maintain interdepencies and ensures that the actions of autonomous units reinforce one another.

---

Although it characterizes a state of development, complexity, unlike autonomy, does not sufficiently inform us about the relationship between an organization and its elements. Neither does it hint at "movement." It is useful mainly as a measure for classification purposes. In *Evolution Management* (1994), in search of a unified process of organizational development, I proposed translating complexity into the "number of interdependencies" between the elements of a social order, an organization. Interdependency between individuals, for example, is not only easier to imagine than complexity, it also represents relationships.

*Framework of movement*

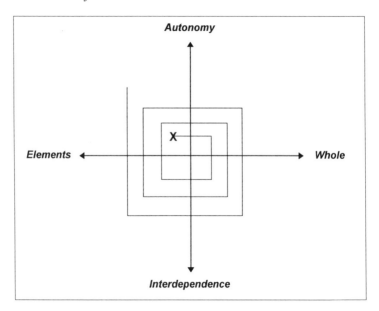

*The development of "organization" is characterized by the oscillating need for autonomy and interdependence of the social order, as a whole, as well as its elements. Organizations, therefore, spiral through the framework of movement when shifting their focus in order to realize their natural growth potential.*

Interdependencies are not necessarily limited to corporate structures. They can also be exercised in virtual spaces such as the Internet. A "virtual company" emerges when a network of individuals agrees on certain interdependencies in order to deliver products and services as a group. In this way, several professional writers in English-speaking countries have formed a "corporation" which offers editorial services to those who surf on the Internet.

Autonomy facilitates innovation and change, whereas interdependence ensures that the activities of autonomous organizational elements reinforce one another. Too much autonomy causes anarchy when organizational elements try to go it alone. Strongly developed interdependence, on the other hand, eventually suffocates internally driven change. Although essential for self-organizing behavior, autonomy and interdependence work as opposite and, at times, paralyzing forces which regulate the relationship between the organization as a whole and its elements. The span of these forces provides a framework of movement which explains the development of organizations from the cradle to the grave. This framework of movement expands the traditional concern of management from the bridging of organizational objectives and individual tasks to the need to direct the antagonistic forces of autonomy and interdependence. No longer can the efforts of management be confined to the mechanical control of the whole and its elements. The forces of autonomy and interdependence, which vary in strength, characterize as much as determine the evolution of existing and emerging social orders. As I shall discuss briefly in the closing chapter, the evolving relationship between autonomy and interdependence causes new organizational forms to emerge although not necessarily within the lifetime of a single company.

The reliance on an internal rather than external perception of reality, also termed "self-reference," represents another key characteristic of self-organizing behavior. In each stage of growth, the position of an organization in the framework of movement and the mental models that underlie the "corporate culture" both determine the view of reality in an organization. Mental models are learned and transmitted by historically developed rituals, symbols, habits and artifacts. These change sluggishly—certainly when compared with the more rapid organizational drift between autonomy and interdependence. Even when the weaknesses of an organizational culture are recognized by each and every employee, it often takes years before they are acted upon. When moving from one growth stage to another, the mental models of an organization simply lag behind those of the organizational elements.

Only after a new direction of change presents itself, do mental models play a role in that they determine the choice of culture-specific measures and strategies. The path of change in the framework of movement, therefore, represents a process of organizational development which depends only partly on culture. A com-

---

*The Domain of Self-Organization*
- *Relativity of Culture*—"Corporate culture" limits the choice of measures that respond to evolving directions of change.
- *Diversity versus Parallels*—In search of growth, "valuing parallels" requires as much attention as "valuing differences." The question should always be: "who happens to be in sync?"
- *Relativity of Leadership*—Leadership deserves a somewhat more modest image. After all, organizations determine the fate of leaders as much as leaders determine the fate of organizations.

---

mon path exists for all social orders which differs only in the pace and span of development.

If cultural diversity is indeed interpreted as different forms of complexity of a unified process of development, then "cultural parallels" must become of paramount importance. Unlike cultural differences which are ingrained through mental models, cultural parallels indicate whether cultures share the same direction of change toward either autonomy or interdependence. Parallels, in other words, refer to conditions where thoughts and behaviors reinforce one another. The dual view of culture, as diversity and parallels, is affirmed by a similar principle of duality in physics. The German physicist and Nobel Prize winner, Werner Heisenberg (1901–76), formulated it thus: "Our world [business society] can be viewed either as divided into different groups of objects [cultural diversity] or as a tissue of events [cultural parallels] in which relations of different kinds [autonomy and interdependence] alternate, overlap or combine and thereby determine the texture of the whole."

The self-induced changes in social orders also encourage us to re-examine the role of leaders. Self-organizing behavior, represented by the inevitable drift between autonomy and interdependence, causes organizations to attract at each stage of growth the leadership needed to exhaust the natural growth potential. When leaders are unable to adjust their style to changing stages of growth, organizations will eventually seek a replacement. In this way, leaders who consolidate and integrate are sought by organizations to replace leaders who have opened up the organization to stimulate the flow of new ideas, and vice versa. Through their self-organizing behavior, in fact, organizations determine the fate of leaders as much as leaders determine the fate of organizations.

### The Question of Evolution

Because self-organizing behavior limits the development of business organizations to their basic design, their "body plan," it is less likely to produce major evolutionary change. Does self-organizing behavior, therefore, impede rather than encourage substantial change?

*Should your organization be focused on autonomy
or interdependence?*

*Has the need for either autonomy or interdependence
dominated the organization?*

*What conditions should be developed to encourage
either autonomy or interdependence?*

*Should the emphasis in your organization be on the whole
or on its elements?*

*Does your organization relate to other organizations
based on their developmental state and needs?*

*Does you organization seal itself off to build up
internal complexity?*

*To what extent has the corporate culture limited
the choice of rules that create change?*

*As Chaos Develops*
*And Organizations Decompose*
*Vision May Emerge From*
*The Fragments Which Shine*
*Through The Whole*

*"On-Board Mechanisms"*
*Should Set The*
*Appropriate Conditions In*
*Unstable Environments*

*

*Chaos often breeds life, when order breeds habit.*
Henry B. Adams

# EMERGING FROM CHAOS

IN A WAY, the unpaved roads in the little villages that flashed by resembled the pathways of our discussion on "evolution." József Dombi, mathematician and professor at the university of Szeged in Hungary, often accompanies me on my way to the airport near Budapest, a trip which takes about two hours by train from Szeged. The not too dominant hum of the train somehow stimulates the flow of ideas and turns a carriage into an excellent meetingplace. Our discussions would generally roam a broad spectrum of topics, from evolution and Umberto Eco's *The Name of the Rose* to management and *The Origins of Order* of Stuart Kauffman.

"I am searching for the meaning of love," József said. In the computer simulations he directed, chromosomes or their mathematical equivalents compete for survival. The survivors need to be recombined to form a new generation of chromosomes, a process referred to as "cross-over." The challenge is to identify on what ground the process of recombination should take place or, in more mundane terms, what mating criteria should be used. Experiments revealed that mating based purely on the gains achieved by each chromosome does not result in a competitive offspring. A combination of gains and "similarity," however, may improve

[ 43 ]

competitiveness. In other words, forming certain species of chromosomes with common characteristics creates a reinforcing effect (resonance) which improves their chance of survival.

Resonance, the reinforcement of characteristics, plays a vital role in the emergence of social orders. But what drives recombination in companies and in how far is timing important?

### *Passing the Threshold to Life*

Try conversing with someone in a crowded place. Often the noise makes a good conversation impossible. Under certain conditions, research has shown that noise does not drown a faint signal but boosts it. Too little noise does not do the trick and too much noise tends to swamp the signal. But the "right" amount of noise pushes a faint signal over a threshold and makes it detectable. The reinforcing interaction between noise and a regular signal is called "stochastic resonance." Stochastic refers to the chaotic or unpredictable character of noise. Resonance refers to the interacting waves. Stochastic resonance occurs only in "non-linear systems." Examples of non-linear systems are a person, a footballer, and an organization. Up to a certain point, a signal has no effect; beyond it, the reaction can be dramatic. First proposed in the early 'eighties, stochastic resonance now causes the Internet search engine Alta Vista to suggest within a second about 30,000 recent articles on its background and application.

In organizations, in certain stages of growth, the noise generated by the internal and external environment also plays a pivotal role in the reinforcement of the signals of inception and decay. In three out of four stages of growth (declining growth, no growth and new growth), the proven tendency of organizations to become more fragmented creates conditions that lead to decomposition. Eventually, recombination of internal and external organizational "fragments" occurs when faint but consistent signals of vision are pushed over the threshold to cognition. Through "reorganizations" which lead up to networks, alliances, joint ventures, spin-offs and management buy-outs rather than blunt lay-off procedures, decomposition followed by the recombination of fragments (individuals and organizations) into new business clusters can be accomplished. Chance comes in when the conditions for new growth are created through "noise" on the divide between organization and society. Management's challenge is to identify and internalize the core parameters which characterize these conditions.

*The Timing of "Chaos" and "Love"*

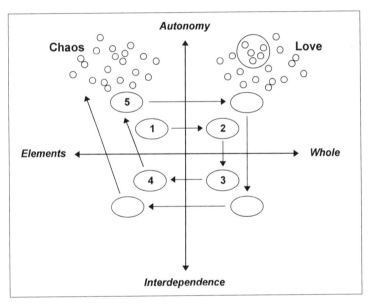

*When growth declines or halts while a state of fragmentation (5) develops, chaotic behavior tends to increase. If the type and amount of "noise" are just right, the faint signals of vision in organizational elements (fragments) are reinforced (1). These visions trigger a "mating process" which recombines organizational elements (both individuals and organizations) into new orders (2).*

Natural growth and self-organizing behavior make the notion of "love," which József Dombi introduced with respect to the issue of recombination, particularly sensitive to timing. Because the framework of movement traces the path of inception and decay, it clarifies where or rather when a certain amount of noise or "chaos" is most effective. In order to explore the timing of chaos, let me briefly evaluate the life cycle of an organization in the framework of movement.

Step 1: An individual or organizational element introduces a vision and its signal is reinforced.

Step 2: The vision attracts and inspires other individuals and organizational elements. A sense of wholeness or "organization" develops which is propelled further by the first signs of growth.

Step 3: As growth develops, the collection of individuals and organizational elements acquires a sense of culture when operational measures, perceived as successful, and events penetrate the mental models to which people subconsciously refer.

Step 4: The individuals and organizational elements determine their role within the whole and how each of them depends on the others.

Step 5: When growth declines, the whole, not able to respond to fundamental developments outside, enters a stage of fragmentation in which individuals and organizational elements start to shift the blame for not meeting the growth expectations. Chaotic behavior will and actually should develop in the fifth step. Its emergence increases the chance that visions are boosted as they develop in the fragments which start to shine through the whole. It is a natural stage to be in.

Although a certain amount of chaotic behavior is widely recognized as crucial for creativity in business, in view of the most recent insights, its timing and also bandwidth, both of which determine its reinforcing character, deserve to be scrutinized with more vigor.

## Responding to Change

With the emergence of chaotic behavior comes the feeling of in-security. Often by spelling out constraints in order to prevent the loss of control, management stifles a natural process of organizational development. Eventually, at the cost of pain, the pressure is relieved by measures such as "right-sizing" which, at that time, are unjustly referred to as inevitable. Although often viewed as a "dark side," chaos is an integral part of business development and a fundamental trait which enables organizations to respond to change.

Medical research has provided remarkable insights into the function of chaotic behavior. For example, the heartbeat of a healthy person may appear stable and regular at first sight yet it shows tiny changes in the timing of each beat which reveal its chaotic behavior. This ensures that the heart is prepared to respond to any change in conditions. To a certain degree, being off-beat serves the purpose of quickly changing the frequency and power of its throbs. Research has also confirmed that just before people die of heart failure, their heart activity becomes monotonous.

In a way, the design of the heart is based on the same principles as that of today's experimental military aircraft which are designed to be inherently unstable. An advanced, on-board computer system is needed to make numerous minuscule corrections just to keep the plane airborne. It is the dramatic price aircraft designers pay to improve maneuverability in order to escape enemy missiles.

The aircraft analogy hints at the need for a shift in the design objectives of tomorrow's organizations. After all, in stages of high growth, when feverishly pumping out products, business organizations develop monotonous behavior. Obsessed by generating revenue through established products, they tend to lose their capacity to respond to fundamental developments in the world outside. The aim, therefore, should be to make organizations at times inherently unstable or nervous but at the same time to employ "on-

*Managing Innovation*

In the late seventies, when electronic reporting networks were virtually non-existent, Texas Instruments implemented a near-perfect reporting and control system across its worldwide organization. The system was designed to manage innovation from the bottom up as well as from the top down. In support of its zero-based budgeting approach which required the yearly justification of all projects, this system controlled the definition and management of investment projects relative to TI's objectives, strategies and tactics. The system, in the end, achieved the opposite of what it was built for. The maze of commitments and the strict rules for the management of innovation made it impossible for TI to react appropriately to developments in the market. It eventually caused the system to become clogged. Innovation, although it needs to be managed, can flourish only when the conditions allow for a certain amount of chaos or nervousness. In this respect, the challenge is to identify the "appropriate" conditions for innovation in each stage of corporate growth.

board mechanisms" which improve the way in which they correct their course. These mechanisms should produce flexible organizations that effectively harmonize with the "rhythm" of evolution, the wobbles of growth. This is not just a matter of changing the organizational structure from, say, hierarchies to networks. As with every complex system, a compound of dynamic factors needs to be explored which leads to well-articulated conditions of business development that are dependent on time and situation. The conditions and the "on-board mechanisms" which manage these in time are discussed from here on.

*Are you suppressing a certain degree of chaos?*

*Should you create a certain degree of chaos to create or sustain growth?*

*Did the search for growth turn your organization into a monotonous machine?*

*What conditions should be created to ensure that the visions of your people shine through?*

*What subtle changes in your organization and business might have a dramatic future impact?*

*When "rationalizing" your organization, did you think only of "decomposition" or also of "recombination?"*

*Vision And Culture
Both Lead To Resonance
And Dissonance*

*They Create And Solve
Business Complexity*

\*

*Culture, then, is a study of perfection, and perfection which insists on becoming something rather than in having something, in an inward condition of the mind and spirit, not in an outward set of circumstances.*
Matthew Arnold

## SEARCHING FOR RESONANCE

CERTAIN "JOGGING WATCHES" can calculate the distance covered based on the number of steps a jogger has made. Before the watch can be used, a jogger needs to establish the average length of his step. Also, a number of test-steps need to made so it can detect and register the typical movements of the wrist when a step is completed. When the jogger is running, the watch will look out for this pattern of wrist movements and count the steps.

In a way, people resemble jogging watches in that they look out for typical patterns and ignore others. According to the international growth conditions survey, for example, managers prefer to focus their organization more on customers and less on products irregardless of the growth stage. Their preferences are in step with the conventional rules of success which emphasize the importance of customers. However important an outward perspective is, these preferences do not correspond with the inward perspective of the actual situation.

Business organizations do open up to customers, but less pretentiously and in a more subtle way. When a persistent decline in growth cannot be turned around, those organizations that have growth potential left do indeed get under the skin of possible customers and temporarily become parasites which feed on hidden customer needs. But, eventually, business organizations tend to seal themselves off when managing their internal complexity. In those cases, as I have witnessed so often, the repeated outcry for customer satisfaction turns into lip service when "selfish" decisions are taken anyway.

Harmonization with the rhythm of evolution, therefore, cannot be achieved by simply applying general rules of success. A more subtle understanding of the internal process of organizational development is needed before an "on-board mechanism" can be designed.

### The Effect of Vision and Culture

In the appropriate environment, faint signals of vision are likely to be reinforced. Generated by individuals, visions may attract and inspire other individuals. Sometimes dormant for years, visions are also pursued through a relentless search for a receptive environment.

Entrepreneurs, as the founder of the Kentucky Fried Chicken

---

*The Spell of Vision*

His vision of preventing the spread of human bondage drove the entire career of Abraham Lincoln, the sixteenth President of the United States. Lincoln encountered major set-backs on the path to realization of his vision. In private life, his commercial ventures failed. After years in Congress, he did not obtain an appointment in the Federal Office. He lost twice in the elections for the Senate, but subsequently was elected President. As President, he searched relentlessly for a general who could end the Civil War. Finally his sixth choice, General Ulysses S. Grant, was victorious.

---

[ 52 ]

franchise, Colonel Sanders, reminds us, may have to present their ideas more than a thousand times before they find fertile ground. Whatever 'vision' itself might be is discussed later in this book but, apparently, it creates the endurance needed to meet the situation and the environment which bears it fruit. Vision not only reinforces the autonomy of its originator but also generates the need for it. Eventually, vision leads to resonance when the thoughts and behaviors of people who are inspired by it reinforce one another. Then "recombination" follows. Recombination actually represents the coalescence of knowledge and ideas which produces business. This process is discussed further in the chapter "When Characteristics Meet, Business Emerges."

Without proof of growth, vision can make people cling together in so-called resonance clusters. When the promise of growth is not realized, however, the clinging power of vision dissipates. Headstrong visions may also start to rule their creators. Some founders of companies, although instigators of remarkable growth, suppress the reinforcement of behaviors and so show themselves incapable of accepting the development of their vision into one that is cherished by the organization as a whole. At that moment, charismatic leaders may become a curse instead of a blessing.

When realizing growth, a resonance cluster, like a jogging watch, registers behavioral patterns which have been shown to lead most successfully to growth. These patterns sustain and, when

---

*Organizational Responsiveness*

The responsiveness of an organization can be expressed as its ability to realize a change in vision in a given amount of time. A headstrong leadership vision as well as a culture which slows down the assimilation of changing views both reduce the responsiveness of organizations.

---

necessary, revive the appropriate conditions for growth. In time, rituals, symbols and artifacts, as mental anchors, are added to these patterns. Also, formal as well as informal policies, procedures and processes are developed which establish abundant operational interdependence.

An integrated "social machine" is eventually created which is capable of generating growth with high probability and minimal risk. "Long-term planning" thrives when growth develops along its typical patterns. Whereas vision creates resonance when it provides autonomy in a collection of individuals, culture generates resonance through the interdependence that develops when high growth is realized. Its emergence demands a different, more enabling kind of leadership which encourages individuals to relate their roles and contributions to those of others within the established patterns of behavior.

At some point in time, as the case of Fokker Aircraft shows, the texture of interdependence may have become incapable of reacting to fundamental changes in the outside environment. New products may have been launched which make the existing products obsolete; leapfrogging technologies may have been introduced by noncompetitors; competitors from remote markets may have entered the market-place; markets may have shifted their interest to satisfy other priorities; macroeconomic parameters may have paralyzed management in the development of organizational responses.

Suddenly, the very behavioral patterns that made an organization excel in meeting its targets may now prevent fundamental change. After all, they developed when realizing rather predictable growth and are not specialized in dealing with discontinuity. When growth continues its decline, resonance turns into dissonance and new visions about fundamental change collide with the established, growth-inspired views of reality in the organization. Departments start to shift the blame and the organizational spirit fragments.

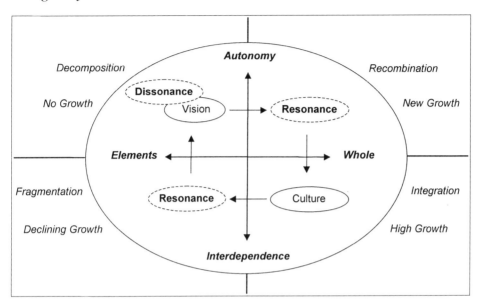

*When its signal comes through, vision may lead to resonance as it attracts thoughts and behaviors which reinforce one another. Culture arises when behavioral patterns which have been shown to lead to growth augment the mental models that people subconsciously use. Culture, in turn, incites resonance when organizational elements identify how their role and contributions depend on those of others in the organization.*

In spite of its negative connotation, however, dissonance is instrumental in the development of business. First, it caps the unbridled growth of complexity and brings it back to manageable proportions. Second, it supports the creation of an environment with the right amount of "noise" necessary for the development and detection of new visions. The "chaos" that is inevitably created demands preparedness, courage and faith to face up to a less predictable future. It is the moment when true organizational "learning" begins in the sense I have defined in the chapter "Mad Interaction."

*Recombination: Preparing for Future Growth*
When it achieved a 10,4% return on capital employed, Royal Dutch/ Shell decided for the decomposition and recombination of key organizational elements. Even after a shake-out of the operating companies which led to a loss of 10,000 jobs, Shell judged its rate of return to be insufficient to sustain the company in the long-term. In 1995, therefore, it broke up its regional and functional management structure and recombined it in five business organizations covering Shell's main activities: exploration and production, oil products, chemicals, gas and coal. According to Shell, these radical changes were needed to prepare it for future growth and a $10bn plus investment program.

## Implications for the Leadership Agenda

The spiral of development in the framework of movement, as the above simplified account shows, is a resonance-searching spiral or "resonance spiral" which is bound to show organizational fragmentation, but not necessarily disintegration, when growth declines. Some organizations, such as Hewlett-Packard, have acquired behavioral patterns that generate growth as well as those that facilitate the process of decomposition and recombination. When a stage of fragmentation is detected, for example, dormant behavioral patterns are activated which will deal with discontinuity and business renewal. To a certain extent, of course, organizational fragmentation can also be sustained artificially in order to create an environment for constant innovation.

In the search for behavioral patterns that fit the needs in the different stages of organizational growth, the "leadership agenda" prompts extension with the following basic learning-points.

• Every organization develops along the resonance spiral and is bound to face fragmentation and, at some point in time, disintegration. The latter occurs when the recombination of organizational elements takes place outside the boundaries of the original organization. As long as they have not exhausted their natural growth potential, however, organizations are able to recombine their organizational elements, thereby maintaining their core identity.

• Each recombination of organizational elements is followed by growth and, eventually, decomposition. Recombination is not limited by the boundaries of the original organization.

• Decomposition naturally caps complexity and brings it back to manageable proportions. The complexity of an organization, in other words, will not necessarily increase forever.

• When growth develops, organizations will produce redundancy as a by-product. The creation of redundancy—that is the accumulation of more resources than strictly needed—is the fourth key characteristic of self-organizing behavior, the other characteristics being: autonomy, interdependence and self-reference.

• The development of self-organizing behavior is characterized by fundamental "development dipoles." Like pendulums, they swing between vision and culture, autonomy and interdepend-

---

*The Force of Management*
Force is determined by organizational inertia and the time it takes to change the responsiveness in each stage of growth.
Management can influence the conditions of change:
• By changing the direction in which a force is exerted either toward autonomy or interdependence.
• By reducing the organizational mass (decomposition), a process which may naturally occur after growth.
• By maintaining some flexibility in the shaping of vision and the culture (see the definition for responsiveness).

---

ence, external and internal focus, integration and fragmentation, growth increase and growth decline, decomposition and recombination.

The resonance spiral, as a *helix of social development*, traces the growth of business organizations from start-up to multinational and back when, in the end, they fragment and decompose. Whatever their size, business organizations are collections of organizational elements, both individuals and groups of individuals, which happen to cling together. They are resonance clusters of resonance clusters.

*Have you found others who share your vision
in one way or another?*

*Exactly who are the people that you need to realize
your vision? What abilities should they have?*

*Is it time to change the vision or should the organization
focus on making it work first?*

*What is the actual responsiveness of your people?*

*In how far does the organizational culture
limit the behavior of your people?*

*Are you experiencing resonance or are you
trying to enforce it?*

*Is your organization fragmenting?
Is it facing a situation of dissonance?
How should you deal with it?*

*Leadership Deals With
The Compulsions Of People
And Organizations*

*When Balancing Between
Autonomy And Interdependence
These Compulsions Determine
Choice*

*

*It is change, continuing change, inevitable change, that is the*
*dominant factor in society today.*
                                        Isaac Asimov


# SENSING DIRECTIONS OF CHANGE

T HE APPROACH OF AA, Alcoholics Anonymous, is to change
people's drinking habit by bringing them together. The
clue to the success of AA is that it assembles people who
share the same problem and the will to rehabilitate. AA, in other
words, creates an environment in which thoughts and behavior
reinforce one another, or resonate. During the rehabilitation process, participants demolish their current behavioral patterns before they recombine thoughts and behavioral elements into a
healthy and growth-oriented way of life. In fact, each person wish-
ing to unfold further his or her own resonance spiral, first redev-
elops a sense of autonomy. Those who have achieved the necessary
change function as examples to the others. They generate the faith
and courage needed to overcome the addiction through a true process of "learning" or internal change.

Following the same principle, the idea in business is to create
resonance by bringing organizations and people together. From a
resonance spiral point of view, organizations and people need to be
in sync and share the drive for autonomy or interdependence.
When they are in the same phase (searching for either autonomy
or interdependence), resonance spirals, each representing a person

or an organization, may connect spontaneously or deliberately to form a string of resonance spirals or a "resonance strand." It concerns a metaphysical type of connection which can be created in a building as well as on the Internet. In other words, by (re)combining people and organizations, leaders create "resonance strands" aimed at autonomy or interdependence. An organization, in other words, is the sum of many resonance spirals, of people, business units and departments, initially driven by vision, later by culture and the realization of growth.

Resonance strands resemble DNA structures which split and recombine. They can be considered as the "social DNA structure." However useful this biology-inspired metaphor may be, business evolution is different from biological evolution. The evolution of business is much faster and driven by spontaneous as well as deliberate forces. The chance that a spontaneous DNA structure mutation will take place in one generation is only one in a hundred million.

The (re)combination of organizations and people is not without risk. The following challenges are typically encountered when resonance spirals are connected:

- *Ill-differentiated "territory."*
- *Cultural differences.*
- *Differences in development speed.*

- *Ill-differentiated territory*—In business, conflicts may develop between companies, organizations and people when they aim for the same rather than complementary "territories." When target territories (and roles) are not distinct enough, colleagues and departments may become enemies. Healthy competition requires an uninterrupted process of differentiation which ensures distinct target customers, product characteristics and operational features. In the search for autonomy, the need for "differentiation" is a pre-

*Resonance Strands*

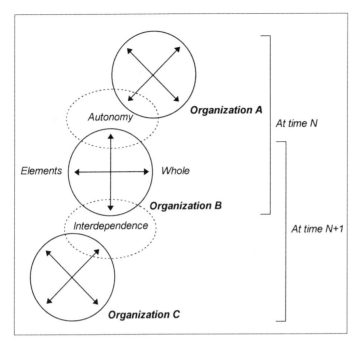

*Organizations and people who share the drive for either autonomy or interdependence are likely to cling together and connect in resonance strands. The development of resonance strands focused on autonomy (at time N) is followed (at time N+1) by the growth of resonance strands in which the search for interdependence is the "clinging agent."*

*Emerging Resonance Strands in the Market*
In 1996, interdependence reflects a changing health-care market. A fragmented customer base consisting of doctors and health centers around the world is gradually clustering into groups that use their power to obtain huge discounts.

requisite for evolutionary selection and survival. It is discussed further in the chapter "When Characteristics Meet, Business Emerges."

• *Cultural differences*—In pursuit of continued growth, companies eventually seek the integration of operational elements inside and outside their organizations in order to streamline the flow of information and goods. In particular, when the drive to link up with internal and external customers, suppliers and partners emerges, organizations come face to face with the need for cultural compatibility. Only when the organizations of these "partners in business" are in sync and share the drive toward interdependence, can differences in habits, rituals and symbols be resolved merely by translation and explanation. The management of cultural issues, therefore, also requires a keen eye for resonance spirals that are in or out of phase.

• *Differences in development speed*—Organizations and people are likely to differ in the speed with which their resonance spirals develop. After all, some will be like Mozart who exhausted his creative potential (in terms of the quantity of catalogued compositions published) in a flash and others will be like Brahms who took almost twice as long to publish a smaller quantity of compositions. As a result, organizations and people who have at first been in sync may later cause a resonance strand to break up. Differences in development speed, therefore, need to be traced and managed constantly.

Because their main challenge is to continue generating (new) growth, leaders must give undivided attention to the formation of resonance strands both inside their organizations and beyond. Not only do they need to know when resonance spirals are out of sync, they also have to set conditions which facilitate the development of new resonance strands and grow existing ones.

### Where Self-organization Meets Choice

When trying to unravel the dynamics of "organizations," the resonance spiral with its typical path of recurrent organizational development is a telling guide. It not only directs the search for characteristic management decisions and organizational behavior, it also helps to identify more precise indicators the use of which goes beyond diagnosis and anticipation. In fact, as the resonance spiral unfolds in the framework of movement, leaders are bound to be confronted with typical "compulsions" which determine the behaviors and directions of change. Along the way, these compulsions produce either autonomy or interdependence.

One of these compulsions is the focus of leadership itself. It is alternating between autonomy and interdependence when it balances between concerns for strategic and operational matters on the one hand and the whole and its elements on the other.

Let me briefly explore how predominant compulsions present themselves in each quadrant of the framework of movement when a business organization develops literally from concept to reality.

- *Top-left quadrant*—Suppose vision comes to the surface in a fragmented environment where it captures the mind of an entrepreneur. The entrepreneurial impulse it creates is reinforced by a compulsion for "identity." The choice is for either personal identity, which reinforces his autonomy, or group identity, which emphasizes interdependence among others. The challenge to develop essentially new business concepts often forces entrepreneurs to distance themselves from common views. This is why entrepreneurs tend to be driven initially by personal identity.
- *Top-right quadrant*—When the efforts of an entrepreneur attract a positive external response, then "alliances" replace identity as the predominant compulsion. Respect for the autonomy of others reflects the tendency to focus on external rather than in-

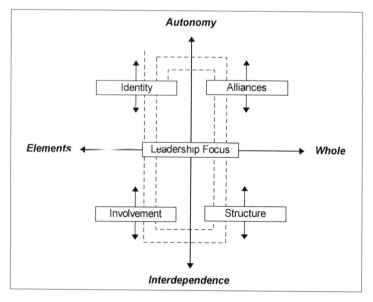

*When the resonance spiral unfolds, several "compulsions", such as* identity, alliances, structure, involvement *and* leadership focus *determine
behavior. For each of these compulsions, the choice is between behavior
which produces either autonomy or interdependence. Behavior and choice
become more complex when an organization grows.*

ternal alliances. It creates openness to other people's ideas and
efforts and brings them in. A constructive exchange follows which
might result in (revenue) growth for the "whole." Growth sets off
a bonding process between the contributing people and organizations and changes the inclination toward measures which focus on
the build-up of internal alliances. The search for internal partner-
ships causes the various cultures to form a "mosaic."
• *Bottom-right quadrant*—When growth continues, operational
processes and procedures, both formal and informal, are established and a web of interdependence develops. The predominant

compulsion changes from alliances to "structure," in particular, structure of accountability and power. In pursuit of growth, the initial drift is toward structure-related measures, such as sign-off and reporting structures, which arrange the entrepreneurial activities. However, when the complexity increases and sub-cultures melt, the development of structure becomes propelled by the need to stay in control of the situation. Focused on the orchestration of entrepreneurial activities at first, structure-related choices now become devices to steer and control an increasingly complex growth-generating machine.

• *Bottom-left quadrant*—When "magic" rituals and symbols spread and a new culture develops, structure is replaced by "involvement" as the predominant compulsion. A tendency to align people and their activities results in measures which ensure that management directions are scrupulously followed up. It represents a response to the need to preserve a situation where the

*Rudimentary Directions of Change*

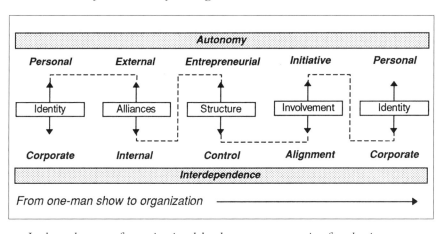

*In the early stages of organizational development, a neat series of predominant compulsions determines the directions of change. Each compulsion deals with two opposite tendencies toward the establishment of either autonomy or interdependence.*

accomplishments of contributing people resonate. To counter possible effects of over-direction, the inclination eventually changes toward measures which seek to mobilize people by encouraging them to develop task-oriented initiatives. Slogans, such as "*You make the difference,*" challenge people to contribute as autonomous individuals.

• *Top-left quadrant* (again)—Eventually, a "living" organization emerges that seeks an identity as a distinct, separate entity. It causes the predominant compulsion to change from involvement back to "identity." To maintain the internal bond, however, the emphasis is put on corporate identity. Then, when for one reason or another growth declines or stops, a new cycle may start. The organization may again fragment, decompose and recombine while waiting for the entrepreneur(s) of its future business to emerge.

The above account, a summary of my appraisal of corporate change in previous work, shows at which moments certain compulsions start to play a role in the various phases of business (and corporate) development. Nevertheless, in the complex setting of reality where organizations consist of other organizations, each riding its own resonance spiral, this simple sequential logic is not sufficient. It fails to identify the subtle differences in leverage between the various compulsions in each stage of growth. Yet, as anchors in social diagrams or "sociograms" in which the evolving organizational conditions are recorded, these compulsions can effectively guide the choice of leaders when they decide on the necessary directions of change.

*Is your organization linking up with partners who are in sync and share the need for autonomy or interdependence?*

*How do you ensure that the alliances inside your organization are in sync?*

*Which strategies are still useful but might have to change in the future?*

*Are the strategies and rules in your organization focused on establishing autonomy or interdependence?*

*Are there conflicting strategies in your organization?*

*What key strategies are required in your organization?*

*Should they be focused on the development of new sources of growth or continued growth?*

*Use Sociograms To Diagnose And Establish The Directions Of Change*

*Business Rules Should Be Derived From Them*

*Rules That Benefit Your Organization*

\*

*Any fool can make a rule… and every fool will mind it.*
Henry David Thoreau

# HEARTBEAT OF CORPORATE EVOLUTION

THE DIAGNOSIS OF heart disorders very much relies on the interpretation of the heart's behavior. An essential yardstick for a physician is the curve traced by an electrocardiograph: the electrocardiogram. It shows the complex movements of the heart as measured by several electrodes.

In a similar way, it should be possible to base the diagnosis of organizational disorders on an interpretation of organizational behavior. However, the complex movements of organizations cannot be traced without identifying first when to measure and compare the behaviors of organizations. As I concluded earlier in the chapter Wobbles of Growth, "through its distinct and recurrent phases of development, growth enables us to transform the arrow of time into a yardstick of corporate inception and decay." Therefore, through its four typical phases (no growth, new growth, high growth and growth decline), growth effectively indicates when to measure and compare organizations in time. In fact, it is not overall growth but rather the various stages of growth which represent the true heartbeat of corporate evolution.

But where should the "electrodes" be placed?

Again, the framework of movement provides guidance. After

all, it not only reveals the self-organizing dynamics of an organization which in itself may consist of other organizations, it also houses compulsions which determine the directions of change. The "electrodes," therefore, are best placed in each quadrant and at the center of the framework of movement where they can measure the forces of the five basic compulsions (identity, alliances, structure, involvement and leadership focus). In this way, they trace the directions of change when compulsions incite either autonomy or interdependence. When plotted in a diagram, the measurements in the directions of either autonomy or interdependence indicate the organizational state. A full cycle of growth requires four similar diagrams, one for each phase of growth.

The diagram can best be characterized as a "sociogram," be-

*The Sociogram and Directions of Change*

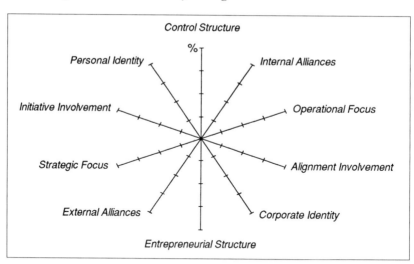

*A sociogram shows the (five) basic compulsions parsed into (10) opposite directions of change which are aimed at either autonomy or interdependence. The distribution of change direction responses or opinions by stage of growth is plotted in a sociogram.*

cause it depicts the social dynamics of a business organization in essentially the same way as a cardiogram depicts the dynamics of the heart.

Through the sociogram, subtle differences in the force exerted by the various compulsions can be made visible from one stage of growth to another. Not only does it increase our insight into corporate dynamics, it is also likely to benefit our influence on the course of organizational development. A more refined sense of direction will improve the effectiveness with which organizational rules are developed. After all, the force exerted by rules, both formal and informal, is, like any other force, sensitive to direction.

### Biased Opinions

The sociogram has been used to reflect the opinions of respondents in the international growth conditions survey. The objective of the survey was to identify tentative patterns of compulsions in each phase of growth which might reveal optimum and adverse situations. Through a questionnaire, respondents, mainly top-level managers, were asked to identify the conditions which best described their company. The questionnaire covered matters such as revenue growth, typical compulsions and the main drivers of change. In this way, 131 managers in 109 companies across seven countries contributed to the survey (see the Appendix for more details). To get a broad representation of companies across industry, the questionnaires were handed out at conferences and, in one country, mailed direct.

The survey outcome, however, forced a reinterpretation of some of its own findings. The tendency of respondents to base their natural views on situations of high growth, as identified in the chapter "Wobbles of Growth," helped to explain unexpected findings about the compulsions of "management focus" and "structure." Respondents seemed to relate "strategic focus" mainly to stages of new and high growth. Apparently "strategy" is associated with the traditional strategic planning process which deals with medium-term and long-term projections in rather predictable circumstances, in particular when growth is experienced. In the questionnaire, however, strategic as opposed to operational focus was meant to refer to situations of structural change in a rather unpredictable world—a situation which coincides with a stage of no growth. Similarly, respondents should have interpreted an "entrepreneurial structure" as something which is needed to achieve fundamental change. Again, the survey results showed the opposite. The entrepreneurial structure of accountability and power flourished in stages of new and high growth. This finding suggested that, apparently, entrepreneurial structures were interpreted as a way to stimulate initiatives focused on exhausting already recognized growth potential in an incremental world. In the evaluation that follows, the sociograms have been adjusted to reflect these findings.

[ 74 ]

## Natural Conditions of Business Development

The respondents were asked to choose from situations which were aimed at either autonomy or interdependence. In this way, they identified both the actual and preferred situations for each compulsion. The perception of reality in the end determines the behavior. The distribution of opinions about the actual situation has survived an evolutionary selection process. The pattern of actual directions of change, in other words, represents the natural situation in each phase of growth.

The appraisal on the following pages discusses these natural patterns and how they tend to change from one growth stage to another, in particular, as a result of self-organizing forces.

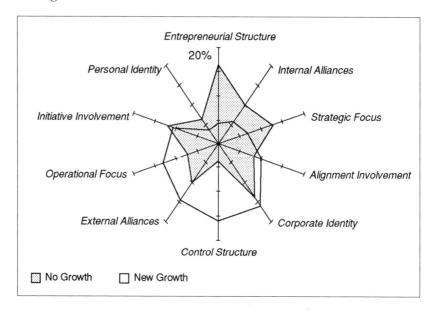

## *From No Growth to New Growth*

During a stage of no growth, fundamental change takes place as one wobble of revenue growth is succeeded by another. It coincides with a strong emphasis on strategic, read structural, change. It also demands that the structure of accountability and power becomes focused on the orchestration of entrepreneurial initiatives. A reliance on internal rather than external alliances establishes internally driven renewal which is so characteristic of self-organizing behavior. In fact, an organization in a stage of no growth has not yet defined its target territories and, therefore, is not yet ready for external alliances. Compared with organizations in a stage of new growth, organizations in a stage of no growth show more compassion for personal identity and initiative.

When new growth emerges, the natural conditions change

visibly. In pursuit of further growth, the emphasis changes to a structure of accountability and power which is more focused on projection and control. As target territories become more distinct, external alliances with suppliers, market-sharing partners and even competitors become feasible. A shift in management attention toward operational issues ensures that further growth is achieved efficiently. With the first signs of growth come subtle changes in the compulsions concerning involvement and identity. With "success" looming, a drift to align people behind the accomplishment of further growth as well as an interest in corporate identity at the expense of the identity of employees becomes evident.

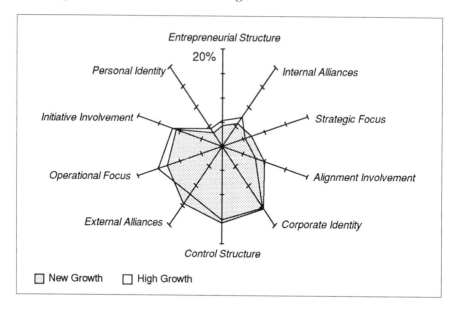

## From New Growth to High Growth

In a state of high growth, the operational focus of management becomes even more important. After all, business processes need to be tuned and improved constantly to maintain a competitive advantage on the market. Subtle shifts indicate that management is increasingly trying to mobilize the internal resources. Internal alliances receive more attention and the initiative and identity of employees gain in importance. Initiative and identity are likely to become cherished as values.

*Uncovering Hidden Potential for High Growth*

In April 1995, Aernout van der Mersch was appointed managing director of CW Lease, a car-leasing company in Belgium. In about a year, his company realized a profit growth of 106%, a motivated staff and a revenue growth of 25%, whereas the market grew only 5.5%. Here is what he did:

- Trust his people to do well (initiative involvement).
- Involve his staff in the development of team objectives (operational focus)
- Agree a common set of rules for internal and external staff (alliances).
- Demand a commitment for the targets set (personal identity).
- Implement a new cost accounting system (control structure).
- Instill a "measure everything" mentality (operational focus).
- Improve quality and price performance (operational focus).

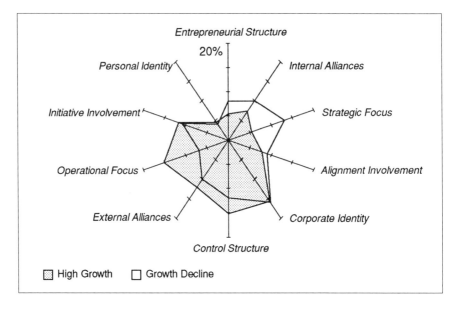

*From High Growth to Declining Growth*

When growth declines, the trend to improve the utilization of internal resources continues. The nervousness of management shows in the subtle change toward alignment which reflects the efforts of management to convince employees of the remaining growth potential that needs to be realized. The organization shows it is becoming more introspective by emphasizing the importance of internal alliances. This introspection coincides with a growing awareness of the need for strategic, read fundamental, change which is marked by a shift toward strategic focus. The structure of accountability and power seeks to mobilize the entrepreneurial behavior needed. Nevertheless, inspired by previous success, the focus on corporate identity is maintained in the hope of keeping the aura of growth alive. It confirms that the principle of business is still based on the "formula" that led to growth in the past.

[ 80 ]

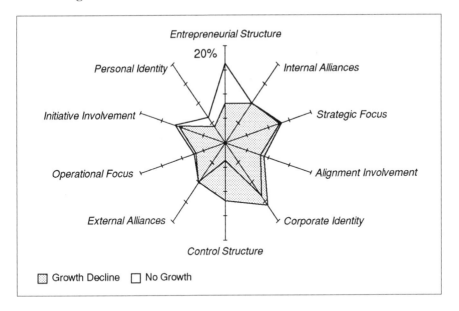

### From Growth Decline to No Growth

When declining growth stagnates, business organizations may be shocked when they realize that the traditional concept of business, which has generated so much growth, is no longer valid. The shock is visible in the receding focus on corporate identity which no longer radiates what it used to symbolize. This shift is compensated by an increase in the importance of personal identity and initiative, the remaining sources of inspiration. To improve the chance of finding new strains of business growth, there is a dramatic shift toward entrepreneur-friendly structures of accountability and power. Designed to cope with unpredictable, unfamiliar worlds, these structures are likely to rely more on what individuals inside and outside the organization can contribute.

## Remarkable Fallacies

Whereas sociograms of the actual situation show the natural conditions of business development, the sociograms with the preferred directions of change illustrate the state of the art in management reflexes. Before elaborating on the background of these patterns, here are some key conclusions that can be drawn based on the survey outcome.

- Not surprisingly, considering previous findings, all preferred patterns of directions of change resemble most the natural pattern of high growth. Apparently, managers hoping to maintain or revitalize growth tend to hang on to conditions which were

*Sociogram: Preferred Change Directions*

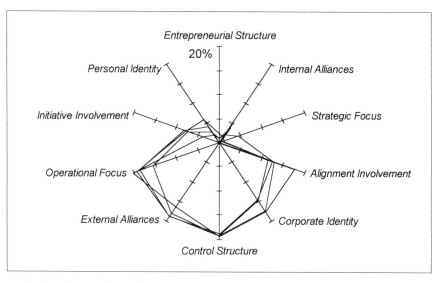

*This sociogram shows the preferred pattern of change directions for each growth stage. It leads to some remarkable conclusions about the assumptions which seem to rule the thinking of managers.*

successful in stages of high growth. This demonstrates a generalizing, indiscriminate view which ignores the specific needs and challenges in other stages of growth.

- The above match, however, is not one hundred percent. Compared with the natural pattern of high growth, all of the preferred patterns emphasize external alliances at the expense of internal alliances. Although a certain "openness" to the outside environment is essential, a single-minded search for solutions externally ignores the basic need of organizations to build internal complexity through a degree of "closure."

- An excessive focus on the alignment of employees combined with a preference for control-based structures demonstrates a rather autocratic bias of management. This tendency directly confronts the widely acclaimed need for coaching and enabling leadership which is inevitable when trying to instill or maintain self-organizing behavior.

What could have caused the development of these reflexes?

Without doubt, one of the primary reasons is the need to produce "growth." Although growth is but the harvest of what has been sown, it remains of key importance to shareholders, stock markets and economies. The longing for certainty and predictability, which still affects shareholders, markets and economies as much as business organizations, restrains the necessary reappraisal of "growth." In future, however, when companies demonstrate the ability to manage their renewal processes, shareholders, markets and economies may become more inclined to open up to the needs of pre-harvest growth stages.

The attitudes of managers are definitely also instilled by the studies of success which are presented in publications and at conferences. The rules in these studies tend to create a rather mechanical and manipulative view of management. Remarkable examples of success, "rule demagogy" and strategies in hindsight inevitably freeze the gaze of managers. As we have concluded before, however, the very nature of evolution prevents management theory being condensed to a fixed set of strategies and rules.

## *When Creating Conditions for Business...*

The framework of movement, the resonance spiral, the compulsions which unfold in two opposite directions and sociograms provide a dynamic perspective of evolving business organizations. Together with the outcome of the survey, they lead to the following conclusions about the creation of the most favorable business conditions.

- The conditions that are established need to resonate with the specific needs of the current growth stage. As the survey indicated, the natural conditions in one growth stage are definitely different from those in another. Not the force of, say, high-growth conditions but self-organizing behavior encouraged by natural patterns makes organizations move from one phase to another. The best self-organizing behavior can be achieved only by the right, growth stage-specific conditions.
- When the heartbeat of corporate evolution stops, the business stops. Success is determined not by high growth alone but also by progress along the resonance spiral, i.e. from phase to phase and from growth curve to growth curve.
- A stage of no growth is as important, if not more important than the stage of high growth. It gives birth to an entire cycle of natural growth.
- The search should be for directions and not for rules. When the directions are set, rules will follow. Directions, the opposite faces of compulsions, apply across cultures and growth stages, while rules are culture-specific and evolve. Indeed, rules are the means of moving organizations in certain directions. But two

companies may decide on different rules in order to move in the same direction.

In creating the conditions for business, the essence of leadership lies in the establishment of the directions of change by growth stage followed by the negotiation of the necessary rules. This process should affect all organizational elements, as they are organizations within organizations with growth cycles and subcultures of their own.

The sociograms with natural patterns can be used to establish the necessary directions of change and to make subtle appraisals in the knowledge that adverse patterns may still rule the minds of some.

*What does "strategic focus" mean to you?*
*Does it concern squeezing out the lemon of predictable growth*
*or does it refer to the creation of structural change*
*toward an "unknown" world of*
*business opportunities?*

*Is entrepreneurial behavior related to the development*
*of initiatives which sustain growth or*
*the search for fundamentally new business?*

*To what extent do the conditions in your organization*
*support its particular stage of growth?*

*Should your organization search for business*
*opportunities and solutions outside or inside?*

*What "on-board mechanism" is in place to mobilize*
*the "hearts" of people in your organization?*

*Should the measure of success in your organization*
*be growth or renewal?*

*To what extent is your organization equipped to*
*deal with stages of no growth?*

*Should you be focused on changing the rules*
*or the directions?*

*The Art Of Creating Business
Is In Finding Characteristics
That Reinforce One Another
Or Resonate*

*Gain Access To The Knowledge
Of People In Your Organization
Through Teams*

*Search For Resonating
Combinations Of Customer,
Product And Competency
Characteristics*

*

*Being good in business is the most fascinating kind of art...*
Andy Warhol

## WHEN CHARACTERISTICS MEET, BUSINESS EMERGES

W HEN A HOUSE is built, the walls are erected only after the foundation has been completed. The roof is constructed last. Once a house is finished, its inhabitants generally do not worry about the foundation.

The word "house" also refers to a business organization—a publishing house, for example. Obviously, building a business also starts with the foundation. This is determined by choices of customers, products and internal competencies. The business is founded merely by combining these building materials. Then the walls and roof are constructed. In business architecture this can be equated with the development of business processes and means. Business processes are concerned with information and material flows, measurement strategies and information architecture. Business "means" refer to operational systems, tasks and organizational structures which, of course, can be identified only when the processes have been (re)designed.

In a growing business, processes and means need constant attention to ensure sufficient operational capacity and to smoothen out unnecessary complexities which affect cost, quality and speed. In an established market where players, customers and products have been defined, these are the three main parameters of distinction left. In the end, although a business organization is generally subject to more change than a house, its "inhabitants" tend to forget about the foundation too.

*High Growth Obsession: Business Foundation Neglect*

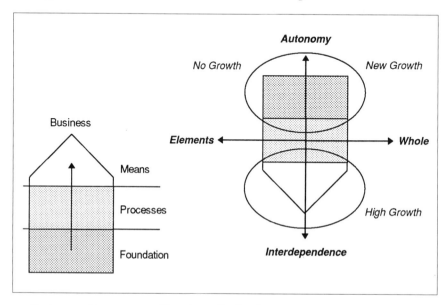

*Business architecture resembles a house. Its foundation, processes and means symbolize the foundation, walls and roof. When growth stagnates and the business has to be redesigned, companies tend to focus on the processes and means rather than on the decrepit foundation. Again, the framework of movement points the way.*

The inclination to choose measures which lead to success in stages of high growth causes the focus to drift to the redefinition of processes and means rather than the foundation of the business. As a result, through methods geared to improve business processes, cost and quality, however important in a growth situation, leaders may either miss the season of opportunity or uproot the seeds of future growth. Then, even after impressive efficiency improvements, they may be confronted with a dying business.

The development of autonomy and interdependence is visible in the build-up of foundation, processes and means. The framework of movement, therefore, also sheds light on the (re)construction of business organizations. Business architecture fits right into it: the business foundation establishes autonomy while processes and means substantiate interdependence. As a result, when the resonance spiral progresses through the framework of movement, it hints at the need to address the business foundation, processes and means. So, each new cycle of growth starts with the adjustment of the business foundation, i.e. the (re)definition of customers, products and competencies.

### Driven by What We "See"

The international growth conditions survey asked respondents in how far customers, products, competencies and attitudes qualify as drivers of change in each stage of growth. The research findings indicate that the opinions are based on a situation of incremental rather than structural change. In other words, change is interpreted in the light of an established business which is realizing its natural growth potential.

- *New growth*—Probably because the first signs of growth become visible when products start to sell, products are seen as the main drivers of change in a stage of new growth. They tend to be tuned until they fit.
- *High growth*—In a stage of high growth, according to the research findings, organizations thrive on all impulses which help further growth to materialize. Customers, products, competencies and attitudes are all seen as drivers of change.
- *Declining growth*—Apparently, when the organization has be-

come more introspective, being caught in its own web of interdependence, products are seen as dim drivers of change.

- *No growth*—In a stage of no growth, business organizations seem to hibernate. Apart from a very faint influence from customers, no other drivers of change stand out. It is as if business organizations with stagnating growth wait for a corporate leader who reconditions them and lights their fuses.

---

*No Rules Are Sacred*

Intergraph, the Alabama-based technical computing concern, which produces drafting software and systems for engineers, took four years to decide on structural change. In the years that followed:

- Products moved from proprietary products to Intel and Windows NT and ended up in a lower price range.
- Typical customer target groups were defined, such as government business, public safety and electronics.
- The organizational side was expanded from engineering to marketing and distribution.

The 1B$ company plowed through a process of structural change which lasted three years and coincided with significant losses. What has been the essence of this process?

---

In reality, when growth declines or stalls, a fundamental process of change should take place. It is characterized by relentless and haphazard trials in which products are tested and competencies are appraised in order to see whether they activate the customers in some way or another. By definition, the target is vague: nonexisting customers, products and competencies—a search which causes Peter Drucker to encourage companies to look for noncustomers.

Companies may take years before they firmly decide to start

this process in which no rules are sacred and the foundation of the business is turned upside down.

### Cross-Differentiation: The Process of Creating Business

Once the foundation of a company has been changed successfully and growth has been restored, the winning strategies and rules are often publicized triumphantly. However good these strategies and rules are, the solution for other companies may be different. What, then, can companies learn from others? Consider, the following "parable" as the start of that discussion.

• *The people*—The growing complexity of society and its increasing wealth caused the needs of individuals to become as relevant as the needs of the masses. People developed an interest in new worlds and alternative realities. Personal choice became important and diverse.

• *The business organization*—Through its modern designs and the rapid introduction of electronic gadgets, it acquired an image of innovation and quality. The drive to miniaturize its gadgets helped it to reduce the cost of manufacturing and distribution and increase the volume of sales. When it launched a new gadget, its distribution network made it possible for people to learn about it across the world.

• *The gadget*—One of the new gadgets developed, which managed to see the light, looked like an ugly duck. It came with simple earphones and did not even have a speaker. In fact, it was too small to incorporate one, but it could play a tape.

• *Interaction*—When this gadget hit the market, it became an immediate success. It seemed to fit the landscape of needs perfectly. It could be carried everywhere and allowed its users to listen to the music of their choice and help them temporarily to create a world of their own.

• *Analysis*—The above parable shows how people, abilities and "gadgets" turn into customers, competencies and products when their characteristics meet, or resonate. In fact, it roughly explains how the Sony Walkman was born.

*Cross-Differentiation: Search for Reinforcing Traits*

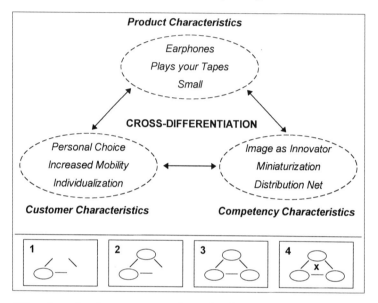

When the traits of customers meet those of products and competencies, new business emerges. Resonance between traits may occur spontaneously but can also be achieved through the deliberate process of cross-differentiation. This reiterative process covers the following steps:

- Search for evolving customer traits, such as needs and factors which hint at areas of customer demand.
- Exploration of product traits, such as features and demand-generating factors, which best support customer traits.
- Identification of competency traits, e.g. capabilities and skills which best meet both customer and product traits.
- Evaluation of clusters of customers, products and competencies of which the characteristics tend to reinbforce one another.

To sum it up, when characteristics meet, new business emerges. Even when traits have evolved quite independently, they may spontaneously reinforce one another. In this way, the electrically powered incandescent bulb, which Edison demonstrated in 1878, started to replace candles, oil, gas and kerosene to light the world when dynamos, fuses and sockets emerged. Propelled by mad interaction, the increasing amount of seemingly unrelated developments invite fusion into new business.

---

*In Search of Resonance*

Increasing unemployment and leisure time (some projections claim that all food and manufacturing needs could eventually be met by 10% of the working population) have triggered a search for new ways to exploit society's unused resources. In command of a major and growing infrastructure, the leisure industry, from cruise organizations to Disney, are compensating for people's lack of daily challenges. Plain leisure is evolving to include courses of all kinds, serious lectures and workshops. The force which drives this trend stems from the deliberate search for product, service and competency characteristics which resonate with evolving societal characterists.

---

Resonance among the evolving characteristics of customers, products and competencies can also be achieved by a deliberate process which identifies customer traits and matches these with product and competency traits following a structured set of steps. Because this process is intended to make unique, or differentiating matches of reinforcing characteristics, I coined the term "cross-differentiation" in *Evolution Management* (1994).

Cross-differentiation is at the core of "creating business." In its broadest sense, it aims at identifying and defining resonating technological, economic and social traits. Due to the great number of possible combinations of traits, choice is essential in this process.

In general, the choice of evolving customer, product and competency characteristics relies on perceptions of markets, products, technology and demand-generating potential.

In several respects, the search for resonance as a way to create new growth in business will affect the business development process.

• *Characteristics create meaning.*—Competencies, customers and products, dominant topics in many management books, become inhibiting rather than enabling factors which tend to limit the view of business people in times of structural change. The questions change from "Who is our target customer?" and "What really are our products and competencies?" to "What characteristics should they have?" Not generalizations about competencies, products or customers but appraisals of their characteristics are needed in the search for new business. After all, people become customers, gadgets become products and abilities become competencies only when their characteristics reinforce one another and sales are generated.

• *Innovation through structure.*—In practice, business innovation is about making unique, resonating combinations of sometimes mundane customer, product and competency characteristics. Innovation, therefore, requires a structured process which manages the complex relationships between evolving characteristics.

• *A different notion of strategic information.*—In business, strategic information which should not end up in the hands of competitors lies less in knowledge about customers, products and competencies and more in the precise understanding of how their characteristics could reinforce one another.

### Creating Business Together

Because of the chance-driven nature of business creation, companies will be forced to fan out the responsibility for the development of new business in their organization. The idea is not only to improve their response to developments in the market and the organization itself, but also to benefit from the broadest possible knowledge gathered through experience.

As a result, methods which give access to the knowledge of people become of increasing importance. However, gaining access is not sufficient. To achieve cross-differentiation, a carefully structured and reiterative brainstorming and evaluation process is required which ensures that ideas about customer, product and competency characteristics induce and, eventually, reinforce one another. Due to the complexity of this task, the use of sophisticated tools will be needed. After all, the number of possible relationships between characteristics is tremendous. As a result, business creation will become more and more a matter of "knowledge engineering."

*Is the basic foundation of the business still valid
in current and future markets?*

*Is your organization mainly preoccupied by
business process issues?*

*In pursuit of future business, has your organization
changed its focus from customers, products and competencies
to customer, product and competency characteristics?*

*How does your organization ensure it traces
and evaluates the impact of the evolving characteristics
and needs of customers and markets?*

*How does your organization translate the evolving market
needs into new product and competency characteristics?*

*How does your organization ensure that
evolving product and competency characteristics are
matched with evolving market needs?*

*Is the organization sufficiently involved in
the business creation process as to ensure
that new business opportunities shine through
the accumulated business knowledge?*

*Suppose your organization knows its customers,
products and competencies well.
Does it also know exactly how their characteristics
reinforce one another?*

*The Purpose
Of Purpose Is
Order*

*Now
Not In The
Future*

*

*We need not only a purpose in life to give meaning to our existence but also something to give meaning to our suffering.*
Eric Hoffer

## THE PURPOSE OF PURPOSE

To COPE WITH new economic and market challenges and, in fact, to fan out the business creation task, the Japanese Kyocera Corporation, a technology company, has divided itself up into 800 small companies. These companies, as organizational elements, are referred to as amoebas. This is not a one-off example. Asea Brown Boveri consists of 1,300 small, quasi-independent units for very much the same reasons. Also, Sony has divided itself into eight companies, each with its own president. The idea behind the increase in autonomy was to maintain the "Sony spirit." In this way, companies are created that consist of many parts, each part being a business organization in its own right and with its own cycle(s) of growth. Capping the size of companies does improve the responsiveness and chance of developing business opportunities. But what is the prerequisite needed to carve out business organizations successfully? And how can they be kept together after the company has been subdivided?

Classical management thinking provides a clear and inspiring answer to these questions: "Each business should have a purpose." Indeed, visionary leaders are often praised for their ability to articulate the purpose of their organization. But how can we explain "purpose" in a world which seems to be driven by mad interaction, a ruthless process of selection and spontaneously emerging social order? Purpose is generally seen as attributing to people a divine quality and role which can hardly be maintained in the light of these evolutionary phenomena.

Then what is the purpose of purpose?

In his book *Darwin's Dangerous Idea* (1995), Daniel Dennett, the American philosopher, offers a revealing perspective in a parable of which the following is but a summary.

*Suppose you decided, for whatever reasons, that you wanted to live in the world 500 years from now. And suppose that in order to realize your objective, you choose to bridge this tremendous stretch of years in a cryogenic chamber which will keep your body alive in hibernation.*

*Apart from the technical issues, assuming that they can be resolved, you are confronted with an immediate problem. Who will keep the equipment running? And where will you locate it? It may well be that in 10 years' time a road is planned right through the building which houses the equipment and your body. If not in 10 years, then perhaps in 50 years. Who will move the equipment? What will happen when the climate or the economic situation changes? War may break out. In 200 years' time, who will obtain the resources needed to keep the equipment going?*

*With these challenges ahead, it seems ideal to construct a giant robot which contains the capsule with your body. A robot, being relatively autonomous, may travel to other locations with better conditions. It must be designed to cope with an evolving society of which the future characteristics are impossible to predict. It may have to negotiate, cooperate and even compete with humans to obtain the resources it needs.*

*Just try to imagine such a creature. Doesn't it remind you of a human? Now, what is the purpose of this robot? When that is clear in your mind, then what could be the purpose of man? Whereas the ultimate purpose of the robot is to carry your body safely into the future, the ultimate purpose of man could very well be to do the same for his genes.*

It is plausible indeed that "genes can be seen to be the original source of [man's] intentionality." What does this make of the divine feeling of destiny which still roams in our minds? What does this make of the teleological management paradigm? And, what does this make of purpose in business?

### Back to Resonance

In order to answer these questions, the problem has to be approached from a different angle. A more basic question has to be answered first: What does purpose do to our minds?

In the brain, information, in the form of electrochemical signals, moves through complex circuits, which are networks of the billions of nerve cells in the nervous system. A single neuron may receive information from as many as 1,000 other neurons. Research has shown that sets of neurons at sites widely separated in the brain fire synchronously in response to certain stimuli. Apparently, when clusters of neurons vibrate in harmony or resonate, we experience the sensations of sight, sound, feeling, smell, recognition and memory. Other research argues that brains, as self-organizing systems, keep their internal activity going through what is referred to as a natural drift, a continuous flux of signals which excites neurons on its way. This view is supported by more recent insights which suggest that consciousness can be explained by signals, so-called efferent signal copies, which loop round and round in the brain.

So, when patterns of neurons are vibrating in harmony, they reinforce one another and resonance occurs. Patterns of resonating neurons are created and sustained through internal and external stimuli. These "resonance patterns" vary in the speed with which they are repeated and cause conscious as well as subconscious sensations. As internal stimuli, resonance patterns excite other resonance patterns on their path as the natural drift progresses. We experience this, for example, when one sweet memory or thought triggers another. In this way, resonance is instrumental in sustaining order in a complex environment of interaction.

Purpose, in other words, can be seen as a means to create and sustain certain resonance patterns which ought to influence our behavior. In order to excite and refresh other resonance patterns, purpose itself must also be a resonance pattern or a complex of resonance patterns. In this light, purpose may be quite unlike what we think it is. It does not necessarily refer to anything divine nor does it deserve the right to let us consciously or subconsciously rely on a mystical goal which justifies our constructive and also destructive actions. In principle, the purpose of purpose is to create and refresh resonance situations in our mind or in a collection of minds, such as a business organization. In practical terms, there is no survival without purpose. This explains why at Sony they insist on maintaining the "Sony spirit."

---

*Order in Complex Environments*
- Resonance is the central phenomenon which creates and sustains order in organizations. It manifests itself through self-organizing behavior.
- Similarly, as resonance patterns in the brain incite other resonance patterns, resonance can be seen to create and sustain order in complex environments of interaction. Also the brain shows self-organizing behavior.

---

To conclude, by articulating purpose, we have a chance of creating and sustaining resonance patterns which may eventually lead to the organizations of the future. Considering our modest role in the process of evolution which is dominated by dynamic phenomena, such as selection, self-organization, chaos and resonance, the potential to create resonance and, through resonance, order tends to be the only possible reflection of our godliness.

*What is the purpose of your business or organization?*

*What is the purpose of your business in the industry and the market?*

*What is the purpose of your business in the eyes of your customers?*

*What should be your purpose?*

*What should be the purpose of your business decades from now?*

*Leadership Drifts Away
From "End-Point Thinking" To
A "Business Evolution Concern"*

*It Must Converge
On Social Engineering,
As Resonance Is The Key
To Growth*

*

*Society is indeed a contract. It is a partnership in all science; a part-*
*nership in all art; a partnership in every virtue, and in all perfection.*
Edmund Burke


# RESONANT SOCIETY


A LTHOUGH THE very nature of evolution prevents management theory being condensed to fixed standards and rules,
several views may have created the contrary impression.
Without pretending to be exhaustive, here are some examples.

As early as 1972, Larry Greiner proposed a well thought through
organizational development model in which stages of evolution and
revolution alternate as companies grow. Five typical phases of development were identified, the first being creativity which is followed by direction, delegation, coordination and collaboration.
Because they identify the typical emphasis in each stage of development, these phases are also prescriptive. In principle, more phases
might unfold as the organization continues to develop. For each
phase, clues to future success are identified by specific rules. For
example, profit-sharing and stock options are used in the fourth
phase. Matrix type organizations tend to appear in the fifth phase.
The model creates order by clustering the rules into five categories,
such as management focus, organization structure, top management
style, control system and management reward emphasis. Greiner's
argument has been based on "the force of history." In fact, he built up
a logic of development phases and rules based on the reasoning that

certain actions cause reactions in time. In this way, Greiner master-fully crafted a model which made sense of the events he observed in various companies. His views still cast a spell on managers and scholars today.

Others have come up with similar models. Richard Nolan and David Croson recently proposed a model with six stages of trans-formation. Keuning, another scholar, inflates Greiner's model to seven phases and wonders what lies beyond.

Both Greiner's model and its derivatives have the following char-acteristics in common.

- *The essence of the work which led to these models revolves around the classification of events as observed in samples of corporate change without the solid backing of an underlying process of natural development.*

*Traditional Models of Development*

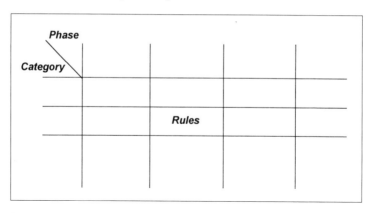

*Traditional organizational development models generally consist of "pre-scriptive" phases and specific rules for each phase which have been clustered into categories.*

- *They are based on the classification of events.*
- *They dictate development phases toward some divine state.*
- *They project general rules on individual companies.*
- *Their practical use is limited.*

Gregory Bateson, the anthropologist who played a major role in the early formulation of cybernetics, warned us not to get carried away by classification but to focus on the process. When Greiner developed his views, however, concepts, such as natural growth, self-organizing behavior, chaos and resonance, had not been articulated to the extent they have been today.

• *They dictate a dogmatic pattern of development phases toward some divine stage.* When companies reach Phase five, then what? The rules that a company invents, adjusts and follows can only depend on the development of its organization and the environment it meets. In other words, considering the process of mad interaction, alternative development situations, other than those suggested, are possible.

• *A general view on the development of organizations is projected on individual companies.* In other words, a macro development pattern is used to explain and judge the development trajectory of individual companies. However, not all organizations will start with the characteristics of the first phase and end with those of the last one. This may explain why an assessment based on the model of Nolan and Croson indicates that most companies have not evolved beyond the first three phases. At first sight this finding is disappointing. But is it meaningful?

• *Managers have trouble identifying in which stage their company really is. As a result, the practical use of these models is limited.* Because the phases of development represent descriptive levels of maturity, good judgment is needed to identify the development stage of a company. When industries become intertwined, such as in the communication, computer and consumer electronics industry, the level of maturity becomes even more difficult to establish. In addition, the rules are not always confined to specific phases of development. Digital Equipment Corporation, for example, has used matrix organizations throughout various phases of its development. And management rewards, such as profit-sharing and stock options, have been used increasingly from the first development stage onwards.

As prophetic statements about the development of organizations, the above models are valuable as situations which illustrate what Greiner refers to as "the developmental perspective." But they are less appropriate as tools to validate and adjust organizations. Their prescriptive nature hinders the development of new rules and limits the criteria by which we judge the state of an organization.

Practical developmental models, such as the framework of movement with the resonance spiral, must be open. They should provide adequate space for the unpredictable trajectory of evolu-

*A Dynamic Model of Development*

| Growth | | | | |
|---|---|---|---|---|
| **Compulsions** | No | New | High | Declining |
| Identity | | | | |
| Alliances | | | | |
| Structure | | **Directions** | | |
| Involvement | | | | |
| Mgt. Focus | | | | |

*The framework of movement, the resonance spiral and its survey-based validation can be traced back to fundamental processes. Its phases of development are measurable and its categories indicate compulsions of which the origin lies in the dipoles of self-organizing behavior* (autonomy versus interdependence, the whole versus elements, fragmentation versus integration, decomposition versus recombination).

tion as a process of mad interaction. They must also be simple, i.e. without too many constraints. Simplicity can only be achieved responsibly if it is based on a fundamental logic which deals with the dynamic perspective. The dynamic perspective, however, is complex and relies on a broad range of phenomena as explored in various sciences. The symbiosis of these findings, therefore, deserves to be a discipline in itself. In the chapter "Mad Interaction," I suggested identifying this discipline as natural economics.

### A Partnership in All Science

As a discipline of research, natural economics aims to explore the inception and decay of social orders, such as business organizations. It is the sum of achievements in various sciences.

Let me summarize the journey that has been made to reach the point at which we now are.

• *The pendulum*—One of the earliest dynamic phenomena which underlies all motion is the pendulum of Galileo Galilei (1564–1642). It led to the development of the clock as we know it now. The awareness of its effect still permeates our society. The resonance spiral, for example, is propelled by pendulum-like shifts between the need for autonomy and interdependence and the whole and its elements. Adam Smith (1723–90) introduced the notion of the invisible hand which manipulates the balancing process between supply and demand. This essentially is a socioeconomic pendulum. Although it has not been discussed in detail, the search for resonance through cross-differentiation is largely driven by Adam Smith's pendulum.

• *Natural growth*—The idea of natural growth has been based on the population growth theory of the British economist Thomas Malthus (1766–1834). In 1845, the Belgian mathematician, P. F. Verhulst, arrived at the first equation which described the tilted S-curve. The development of growth is interwoven with and inseparable from the progressing resonance spiral. The various phases of growth represent the yardstick of inception of decay.

• *Evolution and natural selection*—The ruthless process of natural selection of Charles Darwin (1809–82) or, as Daniel Dennett calls it, "Darwin's blind algorithm of [natural] selection," also determines the emergence of business rules and business organizations. Its impact leads Dennett to the conclusion that Darwin's theory affects our society even more than Einstein's. It has been instrumental in the development of the sobering perspectives of mad interaction and the purpose of purpose.

Darwin's idea of evolution as a gradual process is being challenged. Fossil findings indicate that species may appear abruptly (rather than gradually) and then remain stable for long periods of time in what is called "punctuated equilibria." It has led to a fierce exchange of views between the "guardians of evolutionary theory," such as Dennett, with a gradualist view, and Stephen Gould, who supports the notion of abrupt changes and punctuated equilibria. It is not clear whether resonance has been considered as a way to

*Gradual Change, Resonance, Punctuated Equilibrium?*

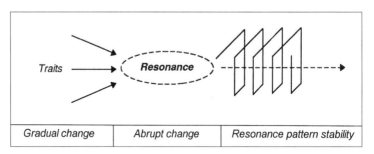

*Tiny changes in the characteristics of species—including those that co-evolve (e.g. bacteria)—and the environment may spontaneously reinforce one another causing an "abrupt" change. The resulting situation of resonance perpetuates itself through cycles in which resonance patterns evoke others in a relatively stable environment.*

explain how minute and gradual changes may start to reinforce one another or resonate so that they lead up to an abrupt change. Because resonance also sustains order, it is plausible to expect it to play a similar role in the explanation of punctuated equilibria.

In any case, as Dennett observes, the central theme in Darwin's book *On The Origin of Species* (1859) is the process of "natural selection" and not the "origin" [nor the "end-point"]. With this hint in mind, I set out in the first chapter "Divine Rules": "The idea [in this book] is to derive rules from an unfolding process rather than from a disputable end-state [success]." In business, however, leaders are still mainly focused on end-points, such as cost reduction. But when reaching them, they often discover that the growth potential of the business has not actually improved. Leadership, therefore, must drift away from "end-point thinking" to a "business evolution concern."

- *Frequency and resonance*—The unit of frequency, the hertz, is named after Heinrich Hertz (1857–94). His name is associated with a quantified measure which allows us to trace the pendulum shifts in time so that their interaction can be studied. When these interactions reinforce one another, they resonate.
- *Uncertainty principle, waves beyond matter, resonance*—Werner Heisenberg (1901–76) introduced the notion that matter can also be explained in terms of waves. In simple terms, where energy waves reinforce one another (resonate), matter manifests itself with a certain probability. Both the notion of resonance in business and the idea of considering cultural parallels in the chapter "Dawning of Movement (Who is in sync?)" have been inspired by Heisenberg's views.
- *Self-organizing behavior*—Since the 1950's, the phenomenon of self-organizing systems has been explored by Ashby, von Foerster, Friedrich von Hayek, Alberto Maturana, Francisco Varela, Gilbert Probst and many others. First discovered in physiological systems

such as the brain, it has been essential in the definition of the framework of movement and the resonance spiral.

• *Chaos*—The phenomenon of chaos not only plays a significant role in the explanation of the resonance spiral. Explored by researchers such as Benoit Mandelbrot, Edward Lorenz, Ilya Prigogine and many others since the 1960's, it explains how minute developments may have a momentous effect on the behavior of chaotic systems, such as business organizations.

• *Stochastic resonance*—It is an insight which explains the unexpected benefit of "noise." First studied by Roberto Benzi, Alfonso Sutera and Angelo Vulpiani in the 1980's to explain the onset of ice ages, now it is emerging as a phenomenon which explains how faint, regular signals can be reinforced by noise. In this way, stochastic resonance seems to explain how vision may emerge in certain circumstances.

### Resonance in Perspective

Teilhard de Chardin, at the time, introduced the "complexity-consciousness continuum" to identify how evolution of more complex brains eventually resulted in consciousness. It allowed the priest, Teilhard de Chardin, to indicate in subtle terms that the evolution of man did not necessarily require an act of God. Based on the conclusions in this book, I suggest making one additional step.

The following parable demonstrates the plausibility of superseding Teilhard de Chardin's notion of the complexity-consciousness continuum by a complexity-resonance continuum. After all, what is consciousness?

*Suppose our planetary system is visited by an intelligent extraterrestrial species.*

*It is very likely that satellites, radar systems and the society of astronomers will be aware of the approaching space vehicles. When the observa-*

*tion is confirmed, the news will go around the world with increasing speed and intensity.*

*Broadcasters, like CNN, will soon inform the world. Governments will start to mobilize the appropriate departments and evaluate the consequences. Companies will seek and create opportunities to make new business out of this situation. Eventually, the earth as a whole will decide on a response in the form of coordinated communication signals, security measures and so forth.*

*The earth could well be perceived as a huge conscious creature. It clearly demonstrates a growing awareness of the presence of visitors and, subsequently, goes through a process of evaluation until it arrives at a more or less coordinated response.*

Does this make the earth conscious?

In fact, what we have here is evidence of resonance patterns spreading over the earth, one triggering the other. So what we see is not consciousness but resonance. We are not dealing with a complexity-consciousness continuum but with a complexity-resonance continuum. The complexity of the earth or, in other words, the interdependence on its surface determines the spread of resonance patterns and, strangely enough, its autonomy.

Resonance forces us to reconsider our divine bias. It keeps us more realistically focused on the continuous struggle for life on the edge of chaos, often, against the odds. Both the search for reinforcing traits and the need for people to be on the same wavelength make resonance a very powerful concept in business society. Through resonance, leadership converges on social engineering when leaders become aware that they must rely on more fundamental processes to generate the conditions necessary for survival and growth.

*Which situations of resonance sustain order
in your organization?*

*To what extent are the standards of success and failure
adjusted when evolving from one growth stage to another?*

*Does your organization regularly evaluate its
state in the light of growth?*

*To what extent are the views on your future business
limited by preconceived forms and structures?*

*Do you sense elements of organizational
"consciousness?"*

*In An Unpredictable World,*
*Questions Are More Important*
*Than Answers*

*Whereas Answers*
*Reflect The Past,*
*Questions Deal With*
*The Future*

*

*If we want everything to remain as it is, it will be necessary for everything to change.*

Giuseppe Tomasi Di Lampedusa

# EPILOGUE

THE LOGICAL APPROACH in this book, chosen to explain the "framework of movement," is misleading in that it does not represent a historical account of how this model has come about. In reality, the framework of movement has been established in quite the opposite way. Its origin stems from a faint pattern which became visible in the evolving landscape of strategic choices in a whole host of companies. The first two of my books on this subject have been accounts of my findings when studying the reports of strategic decisions and the state of the companies in which they were made.

In other words, the origin of my views does not lie in theory but in the sediment of corporate strategies. Through induction rather than deduction, examples revealed their common characteristics which, in turn, pointed the way to the framework of movement. Actually, the theory and links with fundamental processes followed during the search for an explanation. Indeed, once the theory had been identified, it was tested through the growth conditions survey.

The concepts, opinions and conclusions resulting from the survey, although they sometimes only expand classical views, tip the balance of management judgment in a subtle but resolute way. They will change the focus of our mind's eye and affect our views on success, business organizations, the creation of opportunities, the interpretation of organizational signals, the needs of organizations and individuals, the way consultants should do their work and what accountants should recommend to avoid unnecessary risks.

One of the key consequences of these new insights into the inception and decay of business organizations is that processes, rules, standards and judgments have to be tuned to the specific circumstances in each phase of business growth. This tuning process relies on the directions of the basic compulsions in the framework of movement. A separate study for the community of accountants together with the accountant Renes (1996) suggests how the recommendations of accountants on risk management, process control, information & communication and strategic control should change from growth stage to growth stage. In a dynamic environment, in other words, the formal rules and audit standards should also be tailored.

*Business Evolution Management*

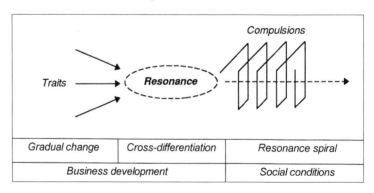

*Business Evolution Management concerns the deliberate search for customer, product and competency traits which reinforce one another and the creation of the most appropriate conditions in each stage of growth.*

Another key consequence concerns the way organizations and people, as self-organizing phenomena, are managed and advised. The emphasis is even more on enabling a process which helps organizations (or individuals) to distinguish the most opportune directions of change on their own. When, based on these directions, the rules and standards of success have been selected and agreed upon, the forces of self-organizing behavior must be trusted to do the work. This crucial shift from prescription to self-interpretation and letting go will affect the way in which the development of the business is guided. Processes and tools are needed to mobilize the organization, enable it to deal with its complexities and to measure its success. In an interactive business exploration workshop, for example, the complex flow of questions and choices will make the use of computer-based tools unavoidable, in particular, when tracing the changing characteristics of customers, products and competencies in order to identify when they reinforce one another (cross-differentiation). In addition, the need to adjust constantly the standards of success will boost systems which enable benchmarking. These systems will function as knowledge engineering tools at meetings as well as on the desktop. In fact, the cases of resonating customer, product and competency traits and the profiles of success criteria will be instrumental in transmitting business knowledge and will become subjects of a lively trade. On the whole, business consulting will make a transition similar to that of leadership from "end-point consulting" to "business evolution consulting."

Ultimately, the unstoppable flow of traditional case studies alone cannot produce an adequate understanding of the origin of growth in business. Within the realm of natural economics, new research projects will emerge which have some dynamic behavioral aspect as their starting-point. Initially, these projects will focus on the fundamentals of change but eventually they will lead to the definition of practical measures and insights. An interesting example is the unusual approach chosen by two researchers at the Erasmus University in Rotterdam. In a working paper for the European Accounting Association (1996), they propose the so-called Gyre-curve to depict how the evolving variety of organizational rules and regulations relates to the evolving variety of external circumstances.

Of the two elements which together describe "learning," viz. differentiation and transmission, differentiation or the exploration of the unknown must take priority over the transmission of "proven rules of success" through case studies and prescriptive models.

# APPENDIX

## Growth Conditions Survey

# GROWTH CONDITIONS SURVEY

*The world is not run by thought, nor by imagination,
but by opinion.*

Elizabeth Drew

1. *Distribution of Responses*
   Number of managers who responded: 131
   Number of companies that responded: 109
   Distribution of responses by country:

| Countries | Belgium | Switzer-land | Nether-lands | Spain | United Kingdom | Other |
|-----------|---------|--------------|--------------|-------|----------------|-------|
| 100% | 2% | 6% | 34% | 44% | 8% | 6% |

2. *Opinions by Company Growth Stage*

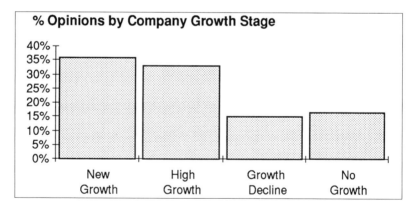

Most opinions suggest that companies experience either new growth or high
growth. Approximately 30 % of all opinions suggest that companies face declining or no growth.

3. *Organizational Fragmentation and Integration by Growth Stage*

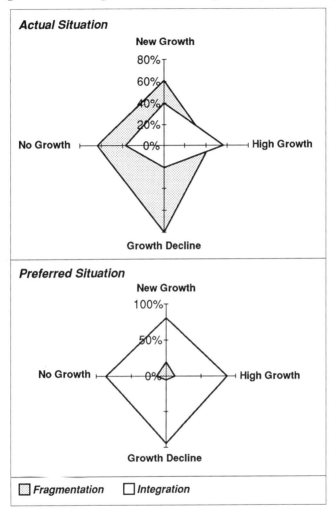

The actual situation represents the perceived reality.
The preferred situation represents the desired reality.
A remarkable difference exists between the preferred and actual situation
which indicates an essential misunderstanding about the way success in business should be achieved.

The preferred situation reveals that managers seek integration in all stages of growth. However good in high-growth stages, the drive to integrate becomes counterproductive when growth declines or halts because it inhibits the necessary freedom needed to develop new sources of growth.

The preferred views of management are generally modeled on the high growth situation.

4. *Drivers of Change by Growth Stage*

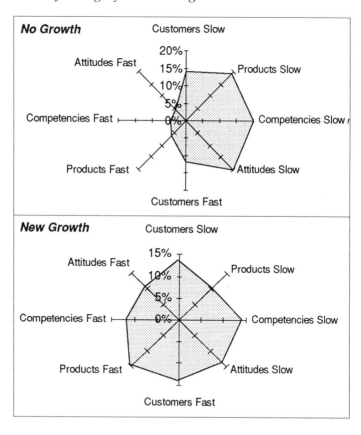

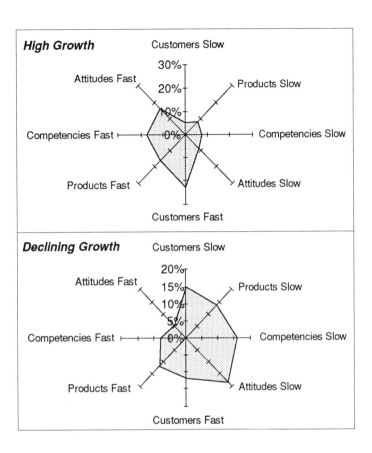

## 5. *Natural Sociograms by Growth Stage*

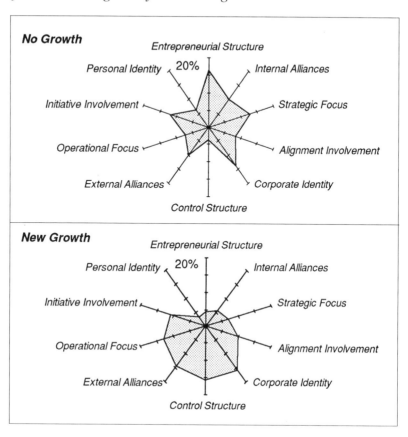

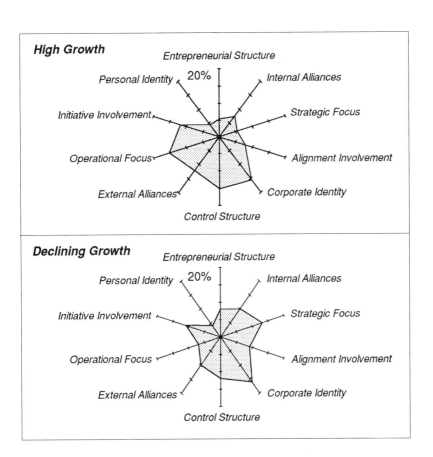

## 6. Preference Sociograms by Growth Stage

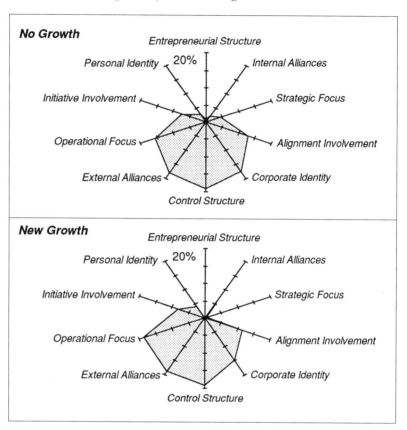

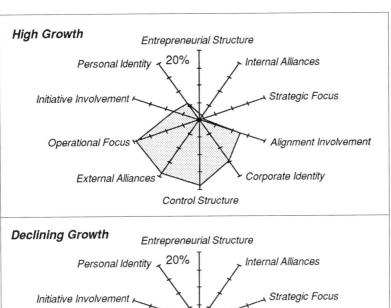

# USEFUL REFERENCES, SOURCES

### General References

Marc van der Erve, *Evolution Management*, Butterworth-Heinemann, Oxford, 1994

Note: *Evolution Management* contains the theoretical framework and references from which this book with its validating survey results has been derived. All chapters in this book draw on it.

Often, the reaction is that revolution rather than evolution is needed in business. In fact, evolution incorporates revolution as an essential state in which gradual changes in traits and the environment reinforce one another.

*Bookshelf '95*, Microsoft

### Prologue

Maarten van den Biggelaar, entrepreneur and owner of *Quote*, the best-selling Dutch magazine on business.

Note: Maarten shared some valuable insights about the structure of this book based on the experience with *Quote*.

ARTICLES:

Tony Jackson, "Now It's a Case of Dumbsizing," *Financial Times*, May 20, 1996

Christopher Lorenz, "A Remedy for Corporate Anorexia," *Financial Times*, October 27, 1995

Stephen Roach, "America's Recipe for Industrial Extinction," *Financial Times*, May 14, 1996

"Giant with Feet of Clay," *Financial Times*, December 5, 1994

### Divine Rules

Peter Drucker, *Managing in Turbulent Times*, Heinemann, Oxford, 1980
Wessel Ganzevoort, Director KPMG MC in the Netherlands, February 6, 1996
> Note: My reference to "a vivid discussion about the inner drive of people in business" goes back to our interesting discussion on the essence of business and its dependence on people. Although our basic premises may have been different, our ideas resonated.

Stephen Hawking, *A Brief History of Time*, Bantam Books, New York, 1988
> Note: We can learn a great deal from other disciplines and sciences.

### Mad Interaction

Daniel Dennett, *Darwin's Dangerous Idea*, Simon & Schuster, New York, 1995
> Note: Dennett's book is a valuable source even for business. It puts our biased views on our existence and future into a sobering perspective. It contains a fierce attack on those who question the gradualism of evolution, such as Stephen Jay Gould.

Stephen Gould, *Bully for Brontosaurus*, Norton and Company, New York, 1992
Stuart Kauffman, *The origins of Order*, Oxford University Press, New York, 1993
> Note: In this rather complex book, Stuart Kauffman reports on his research related to the evolution of organisms. One of the many subjects that Kauffman covers is the dependency of evolution on fitness landscapes. Because it provides so many fundamental insights into evolution, chaos, self-organizing behavior and order, Kauffman's work is also relevant to business and social studies.

Jill and Matthew Ellsworth, *The Internet Business Book*, John Wiley & Sons, 1994
> Note: One of the many books on doing business through the Internet.

ARTICLES:
Robert Barro, "A Rational Choice," *The Wall Street Journal Europe*, October 12, 1995

Andrew Jack, "French Railways Report Angers Unions," *Financial Times*, March 6, 1996

Tony Jackson, "Giant Bows to Colossal Pressure," *Financial Times*, September 22, 1995

Michael Mandel, "Great Theory... as Far as It Goes," *Business Week*, October 23, 1995

Wolgang Münchau, "Lingering Death of AEG," *Financial Times*, December 20, 1995

"Great Expectations, and Rational Too," *The Economist*, October 14, 1995

### Wobbles of Growth

Theodore Modis, *Predictions*, Simon & Schuster, New York, 1992
Note: The inspiring Greek, Theodore Modis, previously a colleague, has valuable insights to offer on the likely development of many phenomena once their natural growth can be observed.

Marc van der Erve, *The Heartbeat of Corporate Evolution*, EM Corporation, Amstelveen, December 1995
Note: This report contains the early conclusions based on the growth conditions survey questionnaires that were returned to me.

ARTICLES:

Theodore Modis, "Life Cycles—Forecasting the Rise and Fall of Almost Everything," *The Futurist*, September—October, 1994

Julian Ozanne, "Koor Reveals New Strategy for Growth," *Financial Times*, March 29, 1996

Louise Kehoe, "Radical Who Built Group with Open Management Style," *Financial Times*, March 28, 1996

Arie van der Zwan, "Vrij van Oude Ballast Kan Fokker Herrijzen," *NRC Handelsblad*, January 24, 1996

### Dawning of Movement

Fritjof Capra, *The Tao of Physics*, Shambala, Boston, 1991
Note: Together with his book *The Turning Point*, *The Tao of Physics* is essential reading on resonance, waves, dipoles in physics and society.

Amitai Etzioni, *The Moral Dimension—Toward a New Economics*, The Free Press, New York, 1988

[ 134 ]

Note: July 12–14, 1996, at the 8th annual conference of the Society for the Advancement of Socio-Economics (SASE) in Geneva, Amitai opened the Communitarian Summit. Both "movements" are his creations. They emphasize the human factor in economic choices.

Friedrich Hayek, *The Fatal Conceit*, The University of Chicago Press, Chicago, 1988

Note: When discussing evolution and movement in society, the work of Friedrich von Hayek is prerequisite reading. His work is packed with remarkably apt insights.

Theodore Modis, *Predictions*, Simon & Schuster, New York, 1992

Gilbert Probst, *Selbst-Organisation*, Verlag Paul Parey, Berlin, 1987

Note: In his latest work, self-organization is drawn into the area of learning, in particular, learning through networking. Seeing relationships, connections and patterns (resonance?) is what generates new urgencies and ideas.

Marc van der Erve, *The Heartbeat of Corporate Evolution*, EM Corporation, Amstelveen, December 1995

Marc van der Erve, *The Power of Tomorrow's Management*, Butterworth-Heinemann, Oxford, 1989

ARTICLES:

Peter Lorange, Gilbert Probst, "Joint Ventures as Self-Organizing Systems," *The Columbia Journal of World Business*, Vol. 22, No. 2, 1987

Chris Thighe, "More Devolution Required," *Financial Times*, March 16, 1996

"Hashimoto's Japan," *The Economist*, January 13, 1996

"Revving Up," *The Economist*, April 27, 1996

### Emerging from Chaos

Alta Vista, the search engine of Digital Equipment Corporation on the Internet.

Note: On practically any topic, it will trace relevant information within seconds. I used it to search for information about stochastic resonance, wavelets and punctuated equilibria.

József Dombi, mathematician and professor at the university of Szeged in Hungary, 1996

Note: József Dombi has produced extraordinary work in the area of neural networking, genetic algorithms and Turing's ID3 algorithm. Relative to the latter, he introduced the so-called "Dombi operator" which, unlike Turing's algorithm, can deal with probabilities.

James Gleick, *Chaos*, Cardinal, New York, 1987
Note: This book really fills you in on most aspects of "chaos."

ARTICLES:

Tom Lester, "Split Up But Still Friends," *Financial Times*, August 25, 1995
"Disorder May Bring a Pattern to Chaos," *Financial Times*, December 7, 1995
"Of Springs, Crowds, Crinkles and the Price of the Yen," *The Economist*, April 13, 1996

## Searching for Resonance

ARTICLES:

David Lascelles, "Barons Swept Out of Fiefdoms," *Financial Times*, March 30, 1995
Stephen Yoder, "How H-P Used Tactics Of the Japanese to Beat Them at Their Game," *The Wall Street Journal*, September 8, 1994

## Sensing the Directions of Change

Marc van der Erve, *The Heartbeat of Corporate Evolution*, EM Corporation, Amstelveen, December 1995

## The Heartbeat of Corporate Evolution

Marc van der Erve, *The Heartbeat of Corporate Evolution*, EM Corporation, Amstelveen, December 1995

## When Characteristics Meet, Business Emerges

Peter Drucker, *Post-Capitalist Society*, Scriptum Books, 1993
Note: On June 16, 1996, at the age of 85, Peter Drucker addressed a gathering in Amsterdam about his views on the post-capitalist society.

Here are some of his remarkable comments: "Do not focus on customers but on non-customers," "Do not become a prisoner of your own market and company" and "Ask the right questions."

Marc van der Erve, *The Heartbeat of Corporate Evolution*, EM Corporation, Amstelveen, December 1995

ARTICLES:

Andrew Baxter, "The Long Road to Battle Fitness," *Financial Times*, June 24, 1996

Paul Betts, "The Birth of the Leisure Ethic," *Financial Times*, June 23, 1996

John Kay, "Oh Professor Porter, Whatever Did You Do?," *Financial Times*, May 10, 1996

### *The Purpose of Purpose*

Francisco Varela, "Two Principles for Self-Organization," In: *Self-Organization and Management of Social Systems*, Springer-Verlag, Berlin, 1984

ARTICLES:

Michiyo Nakamoto, "Sony to Boost Role in Multimedia Markets," *Financial Times*, January 17, 1996

"Artificial Consciousness In the Machine," *The Economist*, April 6, 1996

"In Faint Praise of the Blue Suit," *The Economist*, January 13, 1996

"More in a Cockroach's Brain Than Your Computers Dream Of," *The Economist*, April 15, 1995

### *Resonant Society*

Gregory Bateson, *Mind and Nature—A Necessary Unity*, Bantam Books, New York, 1979

ARTICLES:

Maikel Batelaan and Pim Roest, "Do You Really Have a Transformation Strategy?" *Holland Management Review*, No. 44, 1995

Art Battson, "On the Origin of Stasis," *The Internet*, 1996

Larry Greiner, "Evolution and Revolution as Organizations Grow," *Harvard Business Review*, July-August, 1972.

D. Keuning, "Nieuwe Crises in Organisaties," *F&O*, No. 4, April 1996

*Epilogue*

Marc van der Erve, *Corporate Dynamics*, Sijthof, Amsterdam, 1986

Marc van der Erve, *The Power of Tomorrow's Management*, Butterworth-Heinemann, Oxford, 1989

*Business Evolution Management system Release 3.0*, EM Corporation, Amstelveen, 1996

> Note: In workshop sessions, this Windows 95-based system guides the business development process, records perceptions about future business and helps to define social strategies. It is instrumental to the business planning process.

*BenchMark Release 2.0*, EM Corporation, Amstelveen, 1996

> Note: This Windows 95-based system has been designed to assess any situation based on a set of criteria each of which represents a condition or best practice. It is a simple-to-use knowledge engineering tool which captures the views of experts so that they can be used by others to evaluate and compare people, companies, events and situations.

ARTICLES:

Joop Brukx and Harro Wiekhart, "General Motion Reality Pattern," Rotterdam University, Working paper for the European Accounting Association, 1996

Remko Renes and Marc van der Erve, "Management Control and Evolution Management," Rotterdam University (FMA Conference), June 6, 1996

# INDEX

[139]

[ 142 ]